COHERENCE IN A FRAGMENTED WORLD:

Jonathan Edwards' Theology of the Holy Spirit

Patricia Wilson-Kastner

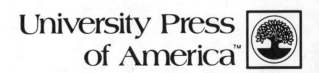

Copyright © 1978 by

University Press of America, Inc.™

4710 Auth Place, S.E., Washington, D.C. 20023

ISBN: 0-8191-0587-2

Library of Congress Catalog Card Number: 78-62667

TABLE OF CONTENTS

To my parents,

who gave me the foundation

which enabled me to grow up and

write this work.

ACKNOWLEDGEMENTS

This work had its beginnings, as do so many others, in a doctoral dissertation written for the School of Religion at the University of Iowa. Out of it came the conviction that although the narrow topic I had explored would not be of general interest, a study of a wider theme in Edwards' theology, that of the Holy Spirit as God graciously uniting all creation in his service and love, might be of interest to a wider audience. Thus, I must give thanks first of all for the patient and painstaking direction of Dr. James McCue, my advisor, and for the support and assistance along the way of others involved in its formation: Drs. James Spalding, Robert Schalemann, Sydney Mead (in whose class the original idea came to light), Orville Hitchcock, and George Forell. My profound appreciation is also extended to others on the School of Religion faculty who generously gave of time and energy in encouraging me on to completion of the task.

In the process of transforming some of my prior work on Edwards into this study of his theology of the Holy Spirit I wish to give special thanks to the following faculty of other institutions: Prof. Thomas A. Schafer of McCormick Theological Seminary in Chicago, who has encouraged me in this project from the beginning; Prof. Sidney Ahlstrom of Yale University, who has helped me with some troublesome points; Prof. Roland Delattre of the American Studies Dept. of the University of Minnesota in Minneapolis, who has offered valuable advice on several occasions.

A first version of this work was tried out as a Lenten series for an ecumenical gathering of United Church of Christ, United Methodist, and Episcopal congregations in River Falls, Wisconsin. For their patience and comments I am exceedingly grateful. I hope that I have been able to incorporate their useful observations.

In the writing of this work I have found great encouragement and assistance from my faculty and student colleagues at United Theological Seminary of the Twin Cities. I am most appreciative of their help, and wish to give particular thanks to the Library staff, especially Dr. Holt Graham, and Ms. Harriet Kruse, whom I incessantly bother with requests for obscure works. For the unfailing aid of our support staff, particularly Ms. Marian Hoeft and Ms. Dorothy Beightol, I am extremely thankful.

Thanks is extended to the following who gave gracious permission to cite from their works: Professor David Lovejoy of the History Department at the University of Wisconsin at Madison for the quotation from Charles Chauncey's "The Heat and Fervor of Their Passions," on page 1; the University of Chicago Press for the citation from Richard Baxter in Alan Simpson's Puritanism in Old and New England on page 2-3; National Councils of the Churches of Christ, from the Revised Standard Version of the Bible, copyrighted 1946, 1952 C 1971, 1973, for the reference to Matthew 22:28-31 on page 35.

Finally, I am appreciative for the support of my husband, G. Ronald Kastner, who as spouse, friend, and colleague has enabled this book to be completed with whatever value it possesses.

If all the books recently written about the Holy Spirit were put into one room together, I suspect we would have the makings of a moderate sized library. Why another book about the Holy Spirit? Of course, one can never have enough of a good thing, and certainly the revival of interest in the person and work of the Holy Spirit is one of the healthiest things that has happened to the churches in a long time. Buy why Jonathan Edwards' theology?

Any one who remembers Edwards at all probably has vague recollections of high school English classes and "Sinners in the Hands of an Angry God," Edwards' powerful revival sermon. Alas, Edwards is a victim of his own success in preaching a sermon which would grasp the congregation's imagination. It is certainly not typical of Edwards' own preaching, for Edwards was much more likely to speak of the glory and love of God offered to us, than to torture us with images of our souls dangling like lost sizzling spiders suspended over the pit of hell.

In truth, Edwards was one of the greatest theological minds America has ever seen, and also one of the most maligned. Over the last thirty years or so, we have seen a substantial revival of interest in his thought, and appreciation for its achievement. What could be more appropriate than in those years when America is celebrating her two hundredth birthday, to praise and study one of our most distinguished Christian thinkers?

Should one struggle through a whole book (or even several) just to memorialize someone? It might indeed be noble to do so, but what difference would it make in our own efforts to understand some of the knottiest religious problems? To study Edwards is no mere antiquarian self-indulgence. Nor is it the glorying in our noble past which moves us to restore and revere past historical monuments such as Williamsburg. So acute was Edwards' mind, and so similar was his time to our own, that his theology speaks directly and penetratingly to our own situation. To investigate Edwards is not only visiting the past, but it is paying a call on a good friend who will give us some helpful advice about what we should do today.

Edwards' lifetime, as I hope will be clear from the first chapter, has a great deal in common with our own. Disillusion with past values and an eager searching for new ideals and experiences were widespread. Many people were rejecting the institutional church, or were experiencing a profound sense of alienation within it. Large numbers of the clergy had grave questions about their faith, and were unable to do more for their flocks than give them lucid sermons about morality and proper behavior towards one another. (Those were the eighteenth century equivalent of the good causes and "pop" psychology talks which pass for preaching in so many churches these days.)

Into this religious disaffection and ennui burst a movement called the Great Awakening. No one person was the founder; in America it represents a current of thought and feeling which was sweeping religious communities in the Western world from Poland and Eastern Europe to Virginia. Because of disputes about true religion, the power of the Holy Spirit, and the gifts and graces of the Spirit, religious people were hotly and fervently divided about what the true Christian church ought to be.

Jonathan Edwards himself was a leader and supporter of the Great Awakening, yet also highly critical of it. He staunchly asserted, on the one hand, that churches ought to believe something and to follow the Gospel, whether or not that was compatable with secular fashions. A personal relationship with God, empowered by the Holy Spirit dwelling within us, is for Edwards the basis of all true religion. On the other hand, he was intensely critical of the judgmental character of those who claimed to be true Christians, and of their attempts to predict the activity of the Holy Spirit (e.g., one had to feel extraordinarily guilty, fall into a faint, speak in tongues, etc.). He undertook the terribly difficult and essential task of attempting to identify the basic principles of an authentic theology of the Holy Spirit, not sub-ject to individual vageries and fancies.

In his attempt to discover the proper balance in his theology, Edwards dwelt with some of the vexing questions which have con-stantly bedeviled theologians, were at the forefront then, and are still with us today. His own approach is, I think, a model of clarity and balance. Which is more important in religion, a clear belief in all the right doctrines, or a good heart and devout life? Some Christians have always valued pure doctrine above all else, asserted that if one believes the right things, the heart will surely follow the head. Others, like Thomas à Kempis, have insisted that it is always much more important to feel compunction than to define it.

From Edwards' point of view neither alone was enough. One must know, in the light of the Scriptures, what compunction is, but one must also practice it. Both mind and heart must be in harmony and symmetry. One must do what one knows is right. Other-wise one is not truly human, in the image of God who is perfect act, but also absolute knowledge. Thus he hoped to counterbalance the strong strain of anti-intellectualism which pervaded the Awakening, and has so strongly influenced American religion since. Edwards would have no part in this truncating of the Gospel, and insisted that mind and heart must work as one, each to its highest power.

Edwards also rejects another false dichotomy which the con-troversies of the Great Awakening exaggerated. Is religion something of a group activity, or is it a personal matter between the individual and God? The old-line Puritans would have claimed that salvation was primarily a matter of God's election of the individual, but that as a consequence of election one had certain obligations. (Even the reprobate had their civil duties, but the elect's were both religious and civil). In their enthusiasm, many of the "awakened" proclaimed that religion was the individual's relationship to the Holy Spirit, and one's duties towards others seemed to consist primarily in exhorting them to be more like oneself.

Neither of these approaches was entirely satisfactory to Edwards. To be chosen by God, to be the temple of the Holy Spirit, was not a solitary affair, but put one in communion with God and thus with all the saints. Salvation was at once the most intensely personal, and at the same time the most profoundly social experience one could have. The saint was a member of a series of inter-relationships which begin and end with God, and encompass the whole world. From this perspective, one can see that an intense personal life of union with God, and a socially active morality not only can, but _must_ exist in the true Christian.

I also highly value Edwards because he places at the center of his theological system a key theological element which has been down-graded by liberal and evangelical Christians alike. Liberal Christianity, at its extremes, turned into an ethical culture group with a good choir on Sunday mornings. Social justice, and later (when the length and difficulty of the struggle became obvious) various sorts of psychological and spiritual self-help systems, have often become goal and gospel for all too many Christians who found God too far beyond their expectations to be worth the effort of investigation. American evangelical Christians have fled from social responsibilities and hidden in a maze of good feeling and self-congratulation that they had accepted Jesus and his salvation. Never mind that nations, and even many of our own people, were groaning in poverty and oppression; send them more Bibles, and comfort them with fond words of the sweet bye-and-bye.

Of course these positions are caricatures, but alas there is enough truth to make most of us uncomfortable. And saddest of all, those who have tried to strike a balance between the two extremes often spent much of their energy congratulating themselves on their virtue in practicing true Christianity. The weakness of all of these kinds of Christianity is that their focus is on ME, my interpretation of the Gospel, social problems, my religious feelings, my ideas and plans to make the world different. I am the source and norm for religion, with a little help from Jesus and the world.

At this juncture, Edwards' theology is extremely important, because he takes ME out of the center of my religious universe and puts in God. I do not ask "Do I accept Jesus?" but "Does God accept me?" My self-improvement is not my most important activity, but my service of God is. I do not ask myself "Am I more faithful to the Gospel than my neighbors?" but "In the sight of God, do I think I am following the Gospel as faithfully as I can?" Once I understand that God and divine grace are at the center of my religious quest, then all the elements of response to God, social justice, and everything else we can think of, will take their place in proper proportion. Edwards tried to think theologically in a way that put God in the center, and us in our rightful place.

Who was this man who produced a theology so balanced and perennially relevant? Edwards was born in East Windsor, Connecticut, October 5, 1703, one of the 11 children of Timothy and Esther Edwards. As a child he was quite precocious, interested in science as well as religion. At the age of 13 (in 1716) he entered Yale, receiving a B.A. in 1720. He remained there for two years studying theology, and then served for two years as a pastor in New York. In 1723 he took an M.A. at Yale, and stayed there two more years as a tutor.

1727 was the date of two momentous events in his life. He married Sarah Pierrepont, who was a spiritual and intellectual companion, efficient homemaker and mother of 11, and charming wife for the rest of their lives. (Sarah died only seven months after him.) He also became the assistant to his grandfather, Solomon Stoddard, the "Pope" of the Connecticut Valley, pastor of the church at Northampton, the most influential church in New England outside of Boston.

In 1729, Solomon Stoddard, who had so long dominated his community, died, and Jonathan Edwards became sole pastor of the Northampton church. Two years later he preached a midweek sermon before the Boston clergy, entitled "God Glorified in the Work of Redemption, by the Greatness of Man's Dependence upon Him, in the Whole of It." This sermon set the theme of Edwards' theological work and preaching in its insistence on the necessity of every and all human beings finding their purpose for life in the glorification of God. It also gave him a reputation among his colleagues as a promising young theologian, who could not be ignored. In the years of 1734-5 he and his congregation experienced a revival of religion, and Edwards wrote his Faithful Narrative of the Surprising Work of God, which made a great impression in Britain as well as America.

The power of the Great Awakening began to stir in the colonies in 1740, when revival movements arose in different parts of the country. Led by such clergy as the great preacher from England, George Whitefield, and the New Jersey Presbyterian Gilbert Tennent, the revivals produced powerful religious experiences among congregations from Georgia and Virginia to Boston. Edwards emerged as a critical supporter, eager to promote its good, but anxious to eliminate its distortions and exaggerations, and the dissension they caused. His own work in Northampton was highly successful, and he wrote several books about the Awakening. In 1746 he authored the most substantive and balanced analysis of the theological issues and pastoral problems involved in the Awakening, in his A Treatise Concerning Religious Affections. He made and sustained a number of contacts with ministers in England and particularly in Scotland, where his written works were read and admired.

In the latter part of the 1740's Edwards' position at Northampton became increasingly uncomfortable. A variety of factors, including economic (Edwards' salary was high and the economy was sagging), social (the New England laity were flexing their muscles and dismissing a great many ministers from their pulpits), and personal (people simply couldn't keep up the emotional high of the Awakening), were involved. The immediate cause was Edwards' insistance that one who was admitted to full church membership and fellowship at the Lord's Supper had to make some profession of personal faith in Christ, and not simply possess a knowledge of some doctrine and exhibit a morally upright life. Edwards was not sufficiently tactful with his lay leaders, and the situation went from bad to worse, with Edwards' dismissal following a very acrimonious dispute in 1750.

From 1751 to 1757 he served as pastor of a small English congregation in Stockbridge, Massachusetts, and missionary to the Housatonnucks who lived nearby. While there he worked with the Indians, and the few white settlers, corresponded with friends abroad, especially certain Scottish ministers, and wrote two of his greatest theological works, Freedom of the Will, and the Great Christian Doctrine of Original Sin, in addition to several manuscripts not published during his lifetime.

The College of New Jersey (later called Princeton) called him to be their president in 1757. Early in 1758 a small-pox epidemic broke out in Princeton, and Edwards, following the model set by other enlightened New England ministers, had himself innoculated as an example to the populace. Unfortunately in the early days of the vaccine physicians were not always able to control the dosage given, and Edwards developed an infection from which he died on March 22, 1758.

His influence was considerable for a time through a generation of disciples who misunderstood him on several crucial points, but kept his name alive. After that, in the United States at least, he was most memorable as the author of "Sinners in the Hands of an Angry God," a revival sermon read by almost every American high school student. In the last few years, as American Christians have tried to recover their own theological heritage, and have sought some alternative to a washed out liberalism or a simplistic evangelicalism, Edwards has been rediscovered. While Edwards is not yet a theological best seller, one may speak of a modest but substantial Edwards revival.

Before we begin together to attend to his theology of the Holy Spirit, I would caution you that I make no pretense to have produced a complete study. Such a work would be several times as long, and probably much more technical in tone. I could, and probably ought to have, referred to many more of Edwards' books and sermons. I have, however, mentioned most of the important ones, and have tried to tell you where to go for more.

I have made an effort to use as many examples as I could when illustrating Edwards' theological position. Almost always they are Edwards'; when they are my own their specific references to present day society will surely make them obvious. You may notice that almost invariably the illustrations chosen have "bite," and relevance. Such is not the case because I have rewritten Edwards; it merely shows that great theology has an enduring quality which speaks to every age.

I. The Outpouring of the Spirit: Edwards and

His Religious Milieu

"Some would be praying, some exhorting, some singing, some
clapping their hands, some laughing and crying, some shrieking
and roaring out; and so invincibly set were they in these ways.....
that it was a vain thing to argue with them....; and whoever
indeed made an attempt this way, might be sure aforehand of being
called an opposer of the Spirit and a child of the devil." [1]

The scandalized author of the lines cited above is not a
contemporary sceptical observer of a particularly excitable and
intolerant charismatic meeting, but the respected Reverend Mr.
Charles Chauncey, an eighteenth century Bostonian minister. In
1742, Mr. Chauncey, horrified at the "indecency of such behavior,"
and lamenting its focus on felt religion rather than on logical
doctrine and more proper moral and respectable behavior, wrote a
stinging critique of that religious movement called the "Great
Awakening." This sudden burst of enthusiastic interest in a
personally experienced religion swept the colonies from Connecticut
to Virginia in the 1730's and 40's, bring in its train as much
controversey as the present day charismatic movement in the
churches, and for many of the same reasons.

To its critics, the "Great Awakening" was at worst the work
of the devil, and at best the deluded ravings of ill-educated men
and weak-minded women and children. To its supporters the "Great
Awakening" was the rousing of the sleeping churches' awareness of
God, an outpouring of God's Spirit which was only the beginning
of God's activity in establishing the divine kingdom on earth.
Opponents attacked every eccentricity of the movement (and there
were many); promoters defended everything that the "Spirit-filled"
person did as divinely inspired activity. Just as our twentieth
century contemporaries attempt to ask what is the value of the
various aspects of different renewal movements in the churches,
so too the thoughtful clergy and laypersons of the eighteenth
century tried to separate the wheat from the chaff in their
renewal movement.

From this mixture of the tangled threads of controversy
Jonathan Edwards, pastor and theologian, tried to weave a coherent
 whole, a fabric of religious life which was both experientially
based, a felt religion, and also intellectually and ethically
responsible. More than any other individual of his age, Edwards
sought to find the value in this outpouring of the Spirit, while
at the same time rigorously testing it in the light of the Scriptures
and the past experience of the church. Edwards always insisted
that novelty was not an argument for or against a practice, but
that the question was: Is it being done in the spirit of the Gospel?

1

To think and act according to the norms of the Gospel was
always Edwards' goal. But in order to appreciate the way he
interpreted and evaluated the Great Awakening in this perspective,
and in the process produced one of the most profound theologies
of the Holy Spirit in Christian history, we must first take a
look at Edwards' religious world, which so influenced his theology,
and at the forces which helped shape that world.

"Demoralized" might be the best word to describe the state of
religion in England and her colonies at the beginning of the
eighteenth century. In the seventeenth century the Established
church felt sure that it had found the right blend of what we today
would call Catholic substance and Protestant principle, and that
the nation's religious life would prosper under this wise blend.
The Puritans, who took a different view of the church's role in the
state, had different hopes for the future. They believed that
beginning with their little "gathered churches" (small groups of
the truly converted) they would be able to establish an earthly
kingdom where the word of God was properly obeyed. Then, because
God's convenant with his people was being rightly kept, God would
act to establish his kingdom on earth. In order to begin this
project for the "new Israel," because the Anglican church would
not cooperate, the Puritans traveled to New England.

There they settled, hoping to be as a "City upon a hill," as
Winthrop observed in his "Model of Christian Charity" preached
to the Puritans as a lay sermon while they were sailing into
Massachusetts Bay. The Deuteronomic saga of God's rewards and
punishments as he tried to make the unruly covenant people into
the godly kingdom of Israel gave the Puritans their model. In
their colony they were sure that the covenant would be observed
and God's kingdom would come to reign on earth. The Puritans, the
"new Israel," did not intend to fail.

When Cromwell and the English parliamentarians established the
commonwealth in England in 1649, both Old and New English Puritans
expected the earthly reign of God to begin imminently. Alas, the
commonwealth and its beautiful hopes were dead by 1660. Now the
"Dissenters," as the Puritans were called, were persecuted and the
ministers deprived of their pulpits. The Established Church had
regained its position of eminence, although now its concern was
to appeal to the broadest number possible, and its theologians fell
captive to the call of rationalism and an emphasis on moral issues
which would be a source of dispute for no one.

The Commonwealth was a failure, and no hope of the earthly
kingdom of God was still left for England. In those sad times the
gentle and irenic Richard Baxter wrote:

  I am farther than I ever was from expecting great matters
  of unity, splendor, or prosperity to the church on earth
  or that the saints should dream of a kingdom of this

2

world.... On the contrary, I am more apprehensive
that suffering must be the church's ordinary lot....[2]

What a great decline in hope since the heady days of the Commonwealth,
when the reign of God was expected to begin on earth any day!

In New England the sense of disappointment ran deep. The
Puritans were greatly distressed at the demise of the commonwealth,
and felt that they themselves had failed in their mission. After
the fervor of the first generation had died, their children were
not so enthusiastic about total dedication to bringing about God's
kingdom on earth. The settled generation was more interested in
building a New England than a New Israel. Thus, a variety of ways,
such as the "Half-Way Covenant" by which one could have one's
children baptized even though one was only a baptized but not full
member of the church, were instituted in order to bring as many
as possible under the church's influence.

A whole new style of sermons developed among New England
preachers. These were the "jeremiads," named after the gloomy
warnings of the prophet Jeremiah. In such sermons, pastors tried
to warn their flocks of the dangers of a covenant not observed,
and tried to call the people back to the early days of their careful
observance of God's law. Recalling to the people their obligations
as a covenant people, and the dependence of the coming of the
earthly kingdom of God on their observance of God's law, the
preachers castigated the congregations for their failure. Each
natural and social disaster was interpreted as a sign of God's
wrath. Although the people listened peacefully, they seem for the
most part to have paid little attention. It is reported that
during one doleful jeremiad, a disgruntled gentlemen blurted out:
"Preacher, don't you know that New England's business is cod, not
God?"

New Englanders were much more enamored of being a prosperous,
respectable, and moral people, than God's chosen people with a
mission leading them to establish God's kingdom. But by the beginnings of the eighteenth century, not only the business minded
laity were questioning the meaning of religion in life. The clergy,
at least in the privacy of studies and quiet discussions, doubted
some of the basic beliefs such as the Trinity which orthodox
Christians had previously taken for granted. Many of the dissenting
clergy in England were Unitarians or Deists, and by the middle of
the eighteenth century, many of the New England ministers would be
espousing the same creeds. Even most clergy who remained orthodox
denied predestination, that cardinal doctrine of Puritanism, and
asserted human freedom to accept or reject a salvation offered to
all. (The Wesleys, for instance, would be included in this category.)

As even the clergy questioned basic doctrines, preaching and
religious life focused more and more on morality and good behavior,
and less on belief. Even if one was not sure whether Christ was
God or not, or just what grace was, all could agree that one ought
not to rob one's neighbor, and ought to pay one's bills on time.

3

Sermons emphasized ethical questions, and tended to be dry formal arguments about behavior. Even on those occasions when the sermon did touch on doctrine, the preachers adopted the same formal approach, assuming that their hearers would be convinced through orderly, logical syllogisms.

Everyone seems to have lost confidence in the old religious views which had inspired the Puritans. Samuel Johnson, a tutor at Yale in 1716 when Jonathan Edwards was an undergraduate there, spoke contemptuously of the works the old Puritan divines had cherished. He called the old orthodox systems "scholastic cob-webs" of English and Dutch theologians who weren't even worth chatting about in the street.[3] In the world into which Edwards was born, it seemed as though Puritan expectations and traditional Christianity were doomed to extinction very quickly.

In their place a new rational and moralistic religion was arising. Newton's physics gave a foundation to this theology, although Newton would have been horrified at this development. Alexander Pope had quipped of the seventeenth century scientist that "God made Newton and all was light." Many agreed enthusi-astically, and tried to use Newton's method to make the moral and spiritual worlds, as well as the physical one, subject to orderly, rational laws. God was understood to be creator who made every-thing according to reasonable, humanly comprehensible laws, and a judge who rewarded nations and individuals (in this life or the next) for good deeds, or punished them for evil. All such notions as the Trinity, Christ's divinity, the person of the Holy Spirit acting in the souls of the saints, predestination, and even the inspiration of the whole Bible were being discarded because they did not fit into this view of the world. "Reason" and "morality" were the watchwords of enlightened eighteenth century Christianity, and this new worldview seemed to be the unchallenged heir to the earthly church, if not to the kingdom of God.

Willing as it was to bury traditional Christianity, including the old Puritan insistence on the Holy Spirit's activity in the world, perceived and experienced by the saints, the Enlightenment did not succeed in its objectives. Puritanism never had completely lost its concern with "inward religion," and by the beginning of the 1730's a spirit of renewal was abroad in the land. Ministers who preached powerfully of the need for inward conversion of the heart as well as intellectual understanding and good deeds had never fallen completely silent in the land. One of the most important was Jonathan Edwards' grandfather, Solomon Stoddard, pastor at Northampton from 1669-1729, under whose preaching the congregation experienced five revivals of intensely experienced religion. Jonathan Edwards, who became his assistant in 1727, and succeeded him in 1729, was thus able to share in one of the earliest of the local revivals, and to find a model of a most effective preacher of "inward religion."

4

The meanings of two words ought to be cleared up at this point. The word "revival" for most of us has connotations of tents and hot summer evenings, of sawdust trails and Bill Sunday style preaching. For Jonathan Edwards and his contemporaries, a revival was simply that, a return to the times at the beginning of their New England history when interest in religion was more fervant. All the notions we have about revivals can be traced back to the extremes of the Great Awakening and especially its following revival at the beginning of the nineteenth century, as these ideas were filtered through our frontier experience. But in this work I shall use the word "revival" as Edwards did, without all its later history. Another term to be clarified is "saint." Most of us, even if we try to be good Christians, would scarcely call ourselves saints. The Puritans, and all the preachers of the Great Awakening, used this term for the converted because it was a Biblical term and it reflected the fact that we are made holy (saints) by God's grace alone, not our merit. We are called Saints, they reasoned, because by grace God has called us to share in his holiness, not because we are holy ourselves.

In 1734, while Edwards was preaching a series of sermons on justification by grace through faith, his Northampton congregation began to experience a renewed interest in personal conversion and transformation of life. Edwards, always a careful observer, analyzed the difference in the before and after states in his flock. He described his parishioners before this sudden interest:

> The great part seemed to be at that time very insensible to the things of religion, and engaged in other cares and pursuits.... Licentiousness for some years prevailed among the youth... there had also long prevailed in the town a spirit of contention...

After this revival of 1734 began, Edwards noted: "Religion was with all sorts the great concern... the eagerness of their hearts could not be hid, it appeared in their very countenances."[4] The earnest behavior of the renewed church members became the topic of conversation from village to village, and soon, spurred by their example, New England was swept with the fervor of "religion of the heart." Presbyterians led the revival movement in the Middle Colonies, and soon the east coast was filled with the "New Light." Refreshed by American and British preachers, among whom was George Whitefield, the great colleague of John Wesley and the friend and admirer of Jonathan Edwards, the revivals continued through the 1740's.

What were these revivals of "vital" or "heartfelt" religion which sparked so much controversy? Why could they cause such great changes in behavior, not only in a few individuals, but among whole towns? What was this "Great Awakening"? Of course the complete answer is extremely complicated, and must be explored on many levels. But the basic point is very simple. Preachers of the Great Awakening returned to the essential Biblical insight which

5

gave Puritanism its power. They asserted that conversion was nothing other than the personal coming of the Holy Spirit to dwell in the hearts of the saints, and that this same Holy Spirit, who gave meaning to individual lives, was the force governing all people and their interrelationships, the destiny of each nation, and the history of the world.

In the broader perspective of history, we can see that this kind of movement was inevitable. Whenever there has been an emphasis on formalism and ritual, the pendulum will swing to a spontanious style of worship. Whether it be elaborate Catholic liturgy or the predictable response of a born-again Baptist, all institutional values tend to standardize themselves, and thus by necessity individual freedom must be curtailed to some extent. Sooner or later people will react against the formality by establishing groups of gathered or charismatic persons who meet above and beyond their institutional commitment, who reform the structures of the church itself, or who leave their church to form a "truer" one. Such were the options in Edwards' day, as they are for us. Edwards and others like him represent the hope for incorporating the power of those movements, critically evaluated, into the greater church. Edwards strove for balance. Renewal movements either fizzle out or are destructive if they are isolated. Happy is the movement with a leader like Edwards, who chose to work within the church for a balanced, constructive harmony!

It would be impossible to overemphasize the emotional power of this message of individual conversion. True religion is not presented as primarily pure doctrine, nor good moral behavior, important as those may be. True religion is neither more nor less than the Spirit of God possessing the whole person. Jonathan Edwards preached this doctrine to his hearers, and shook them into a whole new way of life. Furthermore, Edwards and his fellow preachers insisted, following good Puritan teaching, that if God were truly dwelling in one's heart, he would not hide his presence. Rather, the saint would experience the joy of the Spirit's action in his or her heart and be aware of a communion with God. Old and new blended together in this "Great Awakening." The doctrines were good and venerable Puritan ones, but the strong emphasis on the emotional dimension of religion was new. Connected with this concern for religious affections was a vigorous insistance on the immediacy of the presence of the Holy Spirit in the souls of the saints, and all the effects of that presence. While they too insisted that the Spirit dwelt in the believer, the Old Puritans erected many safeguards against assuming too great a closeness of Spirit and believer. The Awakening tore down many of those barriers. Thus our special concern with Edwards, the greatest theological mind of the Awakening, will be with his doctrine of the Holy Spirit which lies at the center of his theology and that of the whole Great Awakening.

As one might expect about any significant human event, the Great Awakening had many defenders, some of whom went to extremes in their notions of what the Spirit enabled them to do. Opponents of the Awakening, such as Charles Chauncey, denied any validity to the claims of the revivalists to the presence of the Spirit. Others, the small minority such as Edwards, tried to discern the good from the bad in the various manifestations of the Awakening, and while testing the spirits, to hold on to what was good. In order to understand the situation out of which Edwards' theology of the Holy Spirit emerged, we must look at all three of these groups.

For the promoters of the Great Awakening, true religion was primarily the experience of the Holy Spirit acting in the soul. All Puritans, in fact the whole Christian tradition had affirmed that the Holy Spirit was the one who made the Christian holy, bringing forgiveness and sanctification. What gave the Great Awakening its special flavor was its insistence that the action of the Holy Spirit could be intellectually known and emotionally felt by the saint with the same certainty as one could taste the sweetness of honey or touch the hardness of rock. Although the influx of the Spirit could not be merited or forced, it could be prepared for. Thus preachers would exhort congregations in ways calculated to heighten and intensify the hearers' emotions in order to make them receptive to the Spirit. The listeners responded by visible shows of aroused emotions, letting the Spirit within express itself by cries, shouts, tears, dancing, speaking in tongues, exhorting others, and a wide variety of other phenomenon.

Many ministers, such as the Tennents, James Davenport, Samuel Davies, and Isaac Backus, participated in the rousing of souls during the Awakening. Probably the greatest of these preachers was not American at all, but the most popular preacher of his day, George Whitefield of England. Whitefield, a priest of the Church of England, was capable of preaching to up to thirty thousand at a time (as Benjamin Franklin, one of his famous but unconverted (!) friends calculated). Twice Whitefield traveled from England to the Colonies to spread the Gospel to the poor as his colleagues, the Wesleys, had also been doing. He was not only a leader of the revival and a model for its preachers, but he also sparked much of the controversy which surrounded the movement. To his opponents, he was a misleader of the people and a spreader of discord, while to his vast and sometimes tumultuous following, he was an angel of light who spoke only the truth and judgment of God. Benjamin Franklin, although never converted by him, raptly listened to his sermons, and the famous Shakespearean actor David Garrick admiringly asserted that Whitefield could hold a vast audience spellbound just by uttering, "Mesopotamia." More significantly, thousands claimed a renewed relationship to Christ under his teaching.

Whitefield himself described what he hoped would be the results of the Awakening. "Preached this morning in church.

Afterwards, several came to me, inquiring about inward feelings and receiving the Holy Ghost; and I found many begin to be awakened out of their carnal security by the Word preached."[5] The experienced receiving of the Holy Spirit was the great hope of the faithful; it was the indispensible keystone of the Christian life. A good preacher ought to do the proper spade-work to prepare the person to receive God's action by disabusing them of any hope in self, either in their knowledge of God or in their good deeds (carnal security). Only when all hope in self had been given up, and the individual was convinced of his or her unrighteousness before God, would the Spirit be able to come. Once the Holy Spirit did come into the prepared heart, the soul would feel the forgiveness and grace of God, and be filled with peace and joy. Such a converted person, in communion with God through partaking of the Holy Spirit, would do good not out fear of hell or to obey the law, but because doing good was of the nature of a child of God.

How in the world, we immediately react, could such preaching rouse any opposition at all, except perhaps among rationalists who had long since given up any belief in Biblical Christianity? Alas, all human enterprise seem to have some weak point, and the Great Awakening had several. We can find a number of reasons why the Great Awakening was not the answer to every prayer, especially every minister's prayer. Many of the preachers of the Awakening, both clergy and lay (and lay people were allowed to preach and exhort), were not well-educated. They down-graded the intellectual knowledge they did not have, and insisted on an infusion of the Holy Spirit which was accessible to all. We may admire their spiritual democracy, which has since so influenced American Protestantism, but it surely led to some peculiar and downright unbalanced preaching. And, we might add, the socially esteemed and university educated clergy were not willing to admit that the preaching of the miller down the road was more spiritually profitable and truer to the Bible than the sermons the ministers labored on all week.

Vivid and sometimes violent emotions were considered highly desirable and were sometimes deliberately cultivated. Lay and ordained preachers developed techniques for evoking the desired response from their congregations. If others did not have just the same kind of conversion experience they had had, with the same cries, shouts, tears, crying out, and so forth, their conversion was not considered valid by the preachers. Peer group expectation and social pressure determined the style and sometimes the conversion itself.

Because the saints believed that they knew when the Holy Spirit was in them, they felt confident of all their spiritual judgments. They know who was saved and who was not; they were certain what others needed to do to be saved or to be more holy, and, most offensive to the ministers, they publically denounced or praised ministers as good and converted, or as unconverted and therefore unworthy of respect. Thus many a congregation was rent asunder. As the Awakening spread, with its faults as well as its virtues, strong opposition began to unite against it, led by some of the Colonies' most influential ministers.

Charles Chauncey, whose attack on the Awakening we have already referred to, was the most visible leader of the opposition. He was the senior pastor of Boston's prestigious First Church, the occupant of the most influential pulpit on the east coast. Offended by the emotionalism of the Awakening, he attacked the certainty of salvation and the Spirit's presence which the Awakened claimed, and he was particularly offended by the habit they had of judging the spiritual state of lay and clergy alike. By the mid 1740's his articulate voice was joined by the equally eloquent and eminent faculty at Harvard, who resented Whitefield's broadsides at them for making religion a matter of the head and not the heart. They labeled him "...an uncharitable, censorious, and slanderous man," because he had claimed, on the basis of his direct communication with the Holy Spirit, to know that we are in a state of spiritual darkness. Did not Mr. Whitefield know, they asked, that four times a year a committee of "godly ministers" come to the college to check on their good behavior and obedience to the laws of the Scripture?[6] Whitefield seems not to have been very impressed.

Chauncey and others, as time went by, had other grounds for complaint about the Awakening. Did it really have any long lasting effect on people, or was it just a passing emotional fancy, lasting as long as the emotional high could be artificially sustained, but not having any long term effects? It was becoming painfully clear to even some supporters of the Awakening that although emotions might be high and sound very "religious," the Christian behavior of the converted left a great deal to be desired. Many of the "converted" lapsed back into their old ways as soon as the emotional "high" wore off. Enthusiastic gyrations, leaping, shouting and crying out for mercy, and ecstatic reverie about the joys of heaven after proved to be quite transitory phenomena in believers, who soon returned to their former state. What good was achieved, mocked the opponents of the Awakening, if emotions were raised and entertainment provided, but charity not nurtured and long term change not brought about.

Effects of the divisiveness of the Awakening were found all along the east coast. Congregations were split, great figures of the past were derided and their authority denied, and many of the converted seemed to have set him or herself as the unique oracle of the Holy Spirit. As the abuses multiplied and became more obvious, friends of the Awakening often wholeheartedly defended the bad for the sake of the good, and the opposers rejected the whole Awakening and its claim to encourage the "new birth" of the Spirit of God in the believer as being sheer delusion. The illusory character of the movement, they asserted, was proven by the rapid fall of the so-called saints into their previous un-redeemed behavior.

Jonathan Edwards stood almost alone in this controversy. Although a guiding spirit who loved the Great Awakening and who cherished great hopes for it, he also raised a critical voice interpreting and evaluating the Awakening. While the awakened hurled such epithets as "unregenerate" and "damned," and the much maligned critics of the Awakening responded by attacking their adversaries as irrational, deluded, and destructive of the Christian community, Edwards, from the very beginning of the Awakening, wrote and published a series of works designed to try to distinguish good from bad, and to take advantage of the possibilities for growth and renewal in the movement.[7] Within the colonies even his opponents had to admire Edwards' balance and grasp of a complex situation, and those who claimed the experience of the indwelling of the Holy Spirit found in Edwards an able defender who called them back to a truer mixture of their own concerns with the demands of divine love. English and Scotish evangelicals knew the American Great Awakening as interpreted to them primarily through the writings and correspon-dence of Edwards. Even today, Edwards is admired by their spiritual descendants as the most solid proponent of an intel-lectually responsible religion of the heart. (Concrete proof of their esteem is found in the fact that the most complete edition of Edwards' works presently available is a reprinting of an 1834 edition by the Banner of Truth Trust, a British evangelical group.)

What specifically did Edwards set out to do? He insisted first of all that the Great Awakening had to be judged for what it truly was, not just evaluated on the basis of sometimes mis-leading expressions. For instance, being a good psychological observer, he noted that people intensely involved in an activity may cry out or leap up and down. That does not mean that what they are involved in is good or bad; it simply means that their emotions are overflowing into bodily activity. All persons are wholes, Edwards insisted, and every true idea, for instance, has an emotional and physical dimension... Bodily activity is merely an aspect of normal human behavior, not a gauge for truth or falsity. Thus, he concluded, conversion is not true or false depending on a person's visions or shouts, but on more important considerations of love, joy, and a life lived for God and for others.

He warned those subject to such bodily phenomena that such

10

ecstatic gifts as crying for their sins, visions, speaking in tongues, etc., are gifts for the childhood of the church, not for its maturity. What the church, and each individual in it must have as the never changing bedrock of his or her religious life is love, the supreme gift.[8] Such insistence is not new, of course, because everyone from the Apostle Paul to the great sixteenth century Spanish nun, Teresa of Avila, had been saying the same. The centrality of love, and the indifferent and sometimes misleading character of external phenomena, did however desperately need to be underlined at this time for those on both sides of the controversy.

Love, the center of the Christian faith, was not, for Edwards, a pious abstraction, or a warm feeling in the heart. Love was nothing other than the Holy Spirit, who came to dwell in the elect in order to make them children of God, united to God and acting as his children in the world. Behind all of the frenzied activity, the impassioned preaching, and the hoopla of even the most extreme of the preachers of the Awakening was a fervant, if sometimes misguided, search for the Holy Spirit. The pastor, Edwards insisted, ought not to quench the Spirit as the proper Bostonians attempted to do, but to guide and purify the search. Much of Edwards' pastoral and theological life was devoted to that task: to seek to know how God's Spirit acted, and to grow in understanding who that Spirit is. Thus, the Great Awakening provided Edwards with the impetus which shaped his life, a search to understand that Holy Spirit who acts among us as persons who live as a community in God's world.

FOOTNOTES

[1] Charles Chauncey, "The Heat and Fervor of Their Passions," in David Lovejoy, ed., Religious Enthusiasm and the Great Awakening (Englewood Cliffs, N. J.: Prentice Hall, Inc., 1969) p. 76.

[2] Cited in Alan Simpson, Puritanism in Old and New England (Chicago: Phoenix Books, University of Chicago Press, 1955) p. 98.

[3] Cited in Herbert Schneider, A History of American Philosophy (New York: Columbia University Press, 1963) pp. 10-11.

[4] Jonathan Edwards, "A Narrative of Surprising Conversions," in Select Works of Jonathan Edwards (London: Banner of Truth Trust, 1965) v. I, pp. 9, 13.

[5] Written on November 24, 1739, George Whitefield's Journals (London: Banner of Truth Trust, 1960) p. 355.

[6] From "The Testimony of the President..." (Boston: 1744) in American Christianity, Smith, Handy, and Loetscher (New York: Charles Scribner's Sons, 1960) v. I, pp. 331-332.

[7] 1737 - A Faithful Narrative of the Surprising Work of God...;
1741 - The Distinguishing Marks of a Work of the Spirit of God;
1742 - Some Thoughts Concerning the Present Revival of Religion in New England;
1746 - A Treatise Concerning Religious Affections;
1747 - A Humble Attempt to Promote Visible Union of God's People in Extraordinary Prayer for the Revival of Religion.

[8] "Notes on the Bible," in The Works of Jonathan Edwards, Edward Hickman, ed., (London: Banner of Truth Trust, 1974; reprint of Bungay, ed., 1834) v. II, p. 800.

II. Conversion and the Spirit: How God Acts In Us

"After this, my sense of divine things gradually increased, and became more and more lively, and had more of that inward sweetness. The appearance of everything was latered; there seemed to be, as it were, a calm sweet cast or appearance of divine glory, in almost everything. God's excellency, his wisdom, his purity, and love seemed to be in everything; in the sun, moon, and stars; in the clouds and blue sky; in the grass, flowers, trees; in the water and all nature; which used greatly to fix my mind... I felt God, if I may so speak, at the first appearance of a thunderstorm... My mind was greatly fixed on divine things; almost perpetually in contemplation of them."[1]

In those words, written in his journal, Edwards described his own experience of the action of God converting him. When the Holy Spirit was present in the soul, all other reality was pale by comparison. "The appearance of everything was altered." Others reported the same kind of experience in other words, as having their lives changed, being born again, being shaken to the roots and made new again. All of them tried to underline one point, a common feeling: that after a certain kind of action of God in the soul, life is never the same again. God converts the person, that is, turns one around towards himself. After that action, life is never the same again. God is always present, things look different, and one's whole life has a new meaning. No longer is the person self-centered and concerned with him or herself; God is the focus and meaning-giver in life.

Christians have always believed in the need for God to convert them. They prayed for the Holy Spirit to enter them and change their hearts and lives to be Christlike. Such a conversion was not just a passing fancy or temporary emotion, but, as Edwards said, it fixed their persons and all their actions on God. Before they had been concerned for themselves; now God was the center of their lives.

What makes Jonathan Edwards' view of conversion so important to understand? To get our perspective, we must go back to the Puritans in the seventeenth century. Before them, most Christians had spoken of conversion more as a process than an event. One was baptized as a child, and by this act original sin was forgiven and the Holy Spirit came to give one the grace which made a person a child of God. Through prayer, the sacraments, and education, the work of the Spirit grew in one, and the Christian life was nurtured. Conversion was not a one shot affair, but a constant process of growth. One could, of course, decline or even fall away completely from the Christian life if one did not respond to God's Spirit working in one.

13

By the time of the Puritans this older emphasis was yielding to increased preoccupation with an individual's own personal experience of God, which could be known and "mapped out" by an alert individual. These people insisted that the God they experienced was Scripture's God who manifested himself in the gathered community. Nonetheless, each individual was supposed to know this God's action personally in him or herself. An important part of this realization was the event of the new birth, the moment when he or she felt God acting within to turn the person to God. Many kept diaries in which they recorded this crucial moment when God's irresistable grace made them one of the elect. They would return time and time again to this happening, in humility, gratitude, and some anxiety lest they have misinterpreted a lesser state for conversion.

Puritans and "pietists" (a more general term for some of the Puritans' Continental contemporaries who also regarded inward religion and personal conversion to Christ as the center of the Christian life) wrote diaries incessantly. We enjoy these diaries as a good way to know individuals and what they really cared about. But the proliferation of diaries also points to the growing sense of individualism of Christians in the modern world. One can scarcely imagine a twelfth century monk or nun holding the minutiae   of his or her religious experience so directly and self-consciously up for examination in the way the Puritans did. The medieval religious would have said: "God's grace acts in me." By deed if not by word, the Puritan said: "God's grace acts in me." With an introspective concern, the Puritan also asked: "How does God act? When? What are some stages of this activity in me? How can I be sure it was God?"

Such emotional involvement with salvation is difficult to sustain with sincerity over a long period of time, especially with large numbers of people. The Puritans managed to maintain their fervor very well, but by the eighteenth century they had lost much of their old spirit, and were quite formalized in their interest in personal salvation. They were, for the most part, more concerned with right deeds than an upright heart. Much of the force of the Great Awakening was the challenge it raised to return to the original power of the Puritans, their insistence on the individual's encounter with God's saving grace.

Edwards, in his Narrative of Surprising Conversions, relates the dramatic transformation of his congregation when they were awakened by the sense of their own sin and God's mercy to them. He insisted on both the universality and the lasting-ness of God's action. All sorts of people were converted (both men and women in equal numbers!), and this conversion did not dissipate, but was borne out over a long period of time in a variety of charitable works in their lives. Northampton's "quality of life," we today might say, improved because of the people who had been truly converted. Although Edwards was quite methodical in recognizing that certain insights and developments were essential in conversion, he was equally careful to guard God's freedom in working with individuals using different means and evoking a range of emotions with various intensities. Although some of the more extreme preachers of the Awakening presented certain patterns of conversion to their hearers, Edwards was always cautious in guarding individual relationships with God. As the thoughts and techniques of the Awakening were passed on to the frontier revivalists and their twentieth century descendants, the hardliners were listened to, and not Edwards. Edwards' flexibility and sensitivity to the individual, whose personality with all sorts of other factors affecting him or her had to be taken into account, were lost. What was retained of Edwards' view was the importance of the event of conversion, and basic stages of this conversion.

It would be impossible to overestimate the significance of this approach to conversion in the continuing life of American Protestantism. After a brief time around the Revolutionary War period, during which the original excitement of the Great Awakening died down, a new wave of enthusiasm arose during the last decade of the eighteenth century. Under one guise or another, this second Great Awakening would carry the majority of American Protestants into the twentieth century and would influence even those who did not agree with it. The crucial notion which gave life and power to this Awakening was the conversion experience of the individual. The whole mechanism of the successfully growing Protestant denominations was set up to prepare people for conversion, methodically to encourage, and to nurture them through a life "reborn in the Spirit." Preaching and emotional hymn-singing became the form of worship, and sacraments were mere appendages of the devotional life of the churches. (E.g., we wear our "sunday-go-to-meeting" clothes so that we can go to the meeting house to hear the "preacher.")

The nineteenth century revivals evoked similar kinds of responses from ministers as the eighteenth century ones did, but one new factor had entered the picture. In a growing country with a rapidly expanding frontier, Methodists, Baptists, and others who had learned the techniques of the Awakening reached people in great numbers. Presbyterians, Episcopalians, and others who insisted on a learned ministry and a more formal or sacramental worship service simply did not have the personnel or the style to evangelize the unlearned, hard-drinking, and hard living frontier men and women. While the Presbyterian parson was crossing the ts on his Sunday sermon manuscript, the Methodist preacher had evangelized and set up three congregations. At least, so the contemporary saying went.

15

Methodists had learned well the revival technique of emphasis on personal conversion. They (and other popular groups like the Baptists) also made a very significant theological shift. Instead of saying that the Holy Spirit alone could enable human beings to accept salvation, they affirmed human free will, and insisted that humans must of themselves choose to accept saving grace. Conversion became, in the familiar phrase used even today: "I accept Jesus Christ as my personal Savior." This retooling of Edwards' and the first Great Awakening's theology, using its methods, appealing to emotions and focus on personal conversion, but changing the meaning of conversion to an individual's own free decision, was unbelievably successful among the masses of Americans.

One example may be given of the success of this method. In 1800 there were 2,700 Methodists west of the Alleghanies; in 1830 there were 175,000. In only 30 years there were almost 60 times as many Methodists in the West! By 1850, the small Methodist church of pre-Revolutionary days had grown so large that there were 1,320,000 Methodists in the United States, making them the largest denomination in the nation![2] By standards of numerical growth, at any rate, the Great Awakening and Edwards' own theology, had sparked the American religious success story.

Even today the influence of this nineteenth century revivalism is still with us in America. The Southern Baptists, who generally still adhere closely to this style of religion, are the largest single religious denomination in the country. Other denominations, Methodist, Presbyterian, and others, have been influenced by this revivalism in popular piety, type of worship, and theology. Those contemporary religious groups which stress the conversion experience, ranging from independent "Bible churches" to Jesus freaks, are the most rapidly expanding today. But it has been a long road from Jonathan Edwards' pulpit in Northampton to Souls' Harbor in downtown Minneapolis. Having travelled quickly over it, let us return to the source to find out the teaching about our conversion by the Holy Spirit which has so influenced our Protestant churches.

If he could go to one or another of the services of the churches so depending on the Great Awakenings, Jonathan Edwards would probably be shocked and disappointed. While he had focused on personal conversion and demonstrated ways of reaching people at each stage of preparation for, and conversion itself, Edwards moved in a different theological world from the democratic, self-sufficient and individualistic one of the later Awakenings and revivals. Perhaps we, who are more self-conscious in a post-Watergate era of some of the weaknesses of democracy, self-sufficiency, and rugged individualism, can appreciate Edwards' insistance on the uniqueness and centrality of the Holy Spirit's activity as he converts us to become children of God.

In Jonathan Edwards' eyes, the most important part of conversion was God's gracious acceptance of us. We did not first accept him; God empowered us to accept his grace offered to us. The beginning of conversion is to realize who we are and why God alone can save us from ourselves. In a sermon called "Natural Men in a Dread Condition" he warned people about their precarious state before God, while they dwelt comfortably in their sins. (This sermon was a somewhat less graphic version of "Sinners in the Hands of an Angry God.")

Although God had created Adam and Eve so that they and their descendants might be in eternal union with him. God offered Adam a truly free choice of obedience and union with him, or disobedience and separation from God. Adam chose to follow his own desires rather than to obey God, and therefore cut himself off from a relationship with God. Thus, because we were "one moral person with Adam," (a notion Edwards bases on his exegesis of Romans 5) Adam's choice, which was the only truly free choice any human being ever made, cut us all off from a living relationship with God. Therefore, Edwards warns his hearers in this sermon, we are now "destitute of any spiritual good....So the state of natural man tends to that dreadful misery of the damned in hell, because they are separate from God."[3]

We are of ourselves helpless to heal the condition. We are, in Edwards' eyes, like the starving person in the desert with no food, or the terminally ill patient, for whom there is no possible medication. We are helpless to change our state. We can do nothing to earn the love of the God who could save us, because our sin in Adam separates us from God by as wide a gap as that which divided Dives from Lazarus in Jesus' parable. We have not just committed sins; we are in a state of sin. In our present order, all of us are by nature cut off from God. We are by nature no more capable of choosing to relate to God and be his children than a fish is of playing football. Born into a sinful condition, we have only to look about us at our daily actions to see how we ratify Adam's choice by our own acts. We are so little concerned for God and for others, and so much preoccupied with ourselves. Although we look upon someone "far gone in a consumption, or with an incurable cancer" as being "in doleful circumstances," we fail to appreciate our own absolute wretchedness before God, who is the only true source of lasting happiness.[4]

What can we do? Ultimately we can do nothing. God chooses whom he will and rejects whom he will. Edwards on this point was a good Calvinist. God, and God alone controls our destiny as a race and as individuals. Edwards was light years away from the modern day revivalist who would urge us to stand up and make our decision for Christ. He would have apoplexy if he could hear a professedly Christian congregation in the twentieth century singing:

17

> "Are ye able," said the Master,
> "to be crucified with?"...
> "Lord, we are able.
> Our spirits are thine...."

No, Edwards would say, we are not able.... We must receive God's
grace to be enabled to know our condition of being incapable
of following him and knowing him. Only then might God open us up
to himself and make us able. Is there nothing the sinful seeker
after God can do? We can do something, Edwards asserts. We can
try to weed the garden, to prepare ourselves for what God would
have us do. We cannot ever earn or demand salvation, but can
prepare for it, if God has predestined us for it. If we prepare
for salvation we will have a truer understanding of who God is,
and of the great gift he might choose to give us. Salvation is,
after all, the most important possibility in our lives. Thus,
we should be willing to risk everything in making ready for it.
We should be like Noah, who obeyed all God's commands, even though
he did not know what to expect. Do not, he warned his congregation,
be like Noah's neighbors, who heard the hammers of the workmen
building the ark, but took no heed for their own preparations.[5]

In allowing human beings the freedom to prepare for grace,
Edwards was following a long Puritan tradition. This work, which
human beings could do, did not merit or earn salvation. God did
not have to give salvation to those who prepared for grace, although
ordinarily a fervent preparation for grace was one of the signs of
predestination for grace. But a sincere seeking for God obliged us
to prepare, since to simply wait for God to do everything was
sheer presumption.

But, you may ask, as did some of Edwards' questioners, isn't
this preparation which I do really only another way of choosing, and
even earning grace? No, Edwards would say, because the freedom
I am talking about is not on the same level as whether or not I
can go to the barn and unlock the gate. Of course I am free to
choose to do it if I will. What I am speaking of, Edwards would
insist, is our freedom to choose to have God as our saving God,
who loves us and has us as his friends. I can never choose that,
because by Adam's sin we all lost that freedom of choice. Like
the petitioner at the gate, I can only get myself ready, and hope
that the great lord will receive the unworthy supplicant.

It was always possible, although highly unlikely, that God
would dramatically change someone's life, as he did that of Paul
of Tarsus. It was, however, quite unlikely; and sincere preparation for conversion was a divine test of sincerity and an
"ordinary means" for saving grace to enter a receptive heart. Why
must we prepare ourselves? Because God said to. God would give
the seed and the growth if he would; but he expected us to do the
spade work. Not to do so would be to put God to the test, an
action no good Puritan would dare engage in.

18

But suppose that I am a good Puritan and I do prepare myself earnestly and constantly for God's grace. Suppose further that I am one of the elect and God has indeed chosen to enable me to follow him. What will happen when I am converted? Edwards, who had been very interested in science as a boy, retained something of the scientific instinct as an adult. His carefully applied method was to consider what had actually happened in those whose lives seemed to testify over time their truth of their conversion. Although Edwards applied this "case-study" method with himself, and had requested that his wife also write the story of her conversion, his most famous endeavor of this kind was A Narrative of Surprising Conversions, published in 1737. Through it the story of the American Great Awakening was made known in England and Scotland. Both its method of studying cases to deduce the ordinary process of conversion and the conclusions of its author were highly praised by Drs. John Guyse and Isaac Watts (the famous British hymn writer), who wrote the enthusiastic introduction.

In this work Edwards insisted that there are certain common stages that all converted persons go through, but that not everyone spends the same amount of time in each stage, experiences the same emotions, or reaches the stages in precisely the same order. Nonetheless, all the elements must be present or one cannot speak of conversion. Looking back, we can say that Edwards reached this conclusion because he had reduced the theological and psychological elements of conversion to the same bare minimum. We must have a sense of our true condition as sinners, be convinced of God's justice, then begin to see God's mercy and grace in calling us, and finally know the sureness of the Holy Spirit present in us. Edwards' great contribution was not in listing the theological ideas, but in asserting that they were also psycholgoical stages of spiritual growth, and in showing how in specific people this scheme operated.

The first and essential stage is the sense of one's miserable condition by nature and the feeling of urgency that one must quickly escape it and find God. Edwards notes that this first awakening comes in different ways-- some people are awakened quickly, for instance when they hear of another's conversion are "suddenly smitten." Others have been thinking about the matter a long time, and decide that they had better act now. Some had been lukewarmly religious, and finally make up their minds that they need now to be converted. Edwards assures us that there is no one right way; all are ways the Holy Spirit does in fact call people.[6]

We should note that for Edwards and the Puritans generally, this beginning of conversion could come at any time. One case he mentions is of a four year old child, Phoebe Bartlet. (She was still living a good Christian life in 1789, 54 years after Edwards wrote up her case, so we can conclude that he judged her well.)

Phoebe, whose parents paid little attention to her formal religious education because she was, "as they supposed, not capable of understanding," began to pray by herself several times a day. One day her mother heard her praying out loud: "Pray, blessed Lord, give me salvation! I pray, pardon my sins."[7] While Phoebe was surprisingly young for such an experience, the Holy Spirit was inspiring her to see the great truth that was the beginning of conversion: I, by my very birth as a fallen human being, am sinful and unworthy of salvation. Only God can give me this salvation which I need. Phoebe, at a very young age, was a very good Puritan.

The next stage of development is conviction of God's justice in condemning one. The person, who has already recognized that he or she is sinful, admits the absolute justice of God in sending him, her, or everyone together into hell. To us today, this may sound extreme, but we must remember Edwards' profound conviction, which all the evangelicals felt, that because of our fallen state no one is worthy of salvation. "In Adam's fall, We sinned all," said the first New England primer. But this could not just remain an abstract truth; it had to be true for me, so that I could see my relationship to God.

For some, Edwards says, the realization is rather like that of a prisoner who sees his or her condition under the law. Others have a sense of the justice and holiness of God, which induces them to cry out that they are unworthy of God. But no matter what the form, all agree on God's absolute justice in condemning them.[8] Edwards himself, in his recounting of his own conversion, describes how, "from my childhood up, my mind had been full of objections to the doctrine of God's sovereignty." One day he found himself absolutely convinced of God's justice in predestining those whom he would to salvation or damnation. It has taken quite some time before Edwards was able to recognize the "influence of God's Spirit in it," and an essential element of his conversion.[9]

Once this acceptance of God's justice comes, then the individual begins to realize that God does indeed invite him or her to salvation. Such thoughts may be implicit or explicit, strong or weak, and may be bound up with all sorts of doubts and uncertainties. There is "..wrought in them a holy repose of soul in God through Christ, with a secret disposition to fear and love him...."[10] What Edwards is describing is in effect a growth or change process in which the individual moves from a sense of the justice of being condemned rightly by God to an assurance that God will save her or him. The time of this growth process may be short or long, emotionally intense or more placid. Nonetheless, it must take place.

Conversion with assurance of God's salvation is the final stage. In contrast to some of his eighteenth century contemporaries, and the later American revivalist tradition, Edwards maintains that most people cannot name a specific time when they finally were converted. Some, as Edwards remarks, feel conversion as "a glorious brightness shining upon a person.... In others it has been like the dawning of the day."[11] What is common is that for all of them the truths about God and salvation are now real to them and are truths for them. God is their God, and Christ has saved them, and the Holy Spirit is in them. What before was a notional or abstract idea is now the truth of God to them. Even when they suffer from doubts and uncertainty, the light always breaks forth again for them, and they find that God's saving love is the stability in their lives. Though they may question, they are never truly shaken. God is their God, and "nothing can separate us from the love of God in Christ Jesus."

Edwards lifts up the example of a seventy year old woman, who had always been a morally good person, but one day when reading her Bible realized that it was all new to her. "She had often heard of it, and read it, but never till now saw it as real."[12] Besides showing that conversion can come at any age, Edwards here underlined that conversion was not a matter of good works, but of the Holy Spirit changing the heart of the person and turning it towards him. Conversion is God's gracious work transforming the person, not our work changing ourselves.

How, then, does God transform the hearts of the elect? We have read of what happens in the process of conversion from the perspective of human experience. That is, Edwards described the human feelings which develop during conversion. But what is God doing which causes these changes in the individual? In his A Treatise Concerning Religious Affections, Edwards explained what happened in conversion from the perspective of the divine activity. From the Scriptures we learn, Edwards states, that the work of the Spirit of God is giving a new birth, a new principle of life, a new nature. "It is a new foundation laid in the soul." The Holy Spirit gives a new principle of life so that the person can have a new and spiritual nature."[13]

Where before the person was a sinner, "curved in upon himself," (to use Augustine's phrase) separated from God and acting for his or her own selfish purposes, now the person's whole nature is changed. For Edwards, nature meant what the person most essentially was, the core of his or her being from which all thoughts, decisions, and actions spring. Instead of being directed to self, now the converted person has God as his or her ordering principle. God was the focus of life, and the personal source of life and power for the saint. All the pangs of conviction of sin and God's justice were necessary because the old nature was sinful and needed to be replaced. The struggle and joy in conversion expressed the transformation of the person from an autonomous, selfish self to a God-centered person.

Because the converted person has been given the new nature by the Holy Spirit, he or she is enabled to see the truth clearly to have the vision of the truth appear as new and real to him or her. Because the saint was now God-centered, he or she can see the divine dimension in everything. Now the person can perceive the "beauty of holiness" in as real a way as one can taste honey. It enables the saint to behold the glory of God consisting in the beauty of his holiness manifest in everything, "and 'tis this sight only, which will melt and humble the hearts of men, and wean them from the world, and draw them to God, and effectually change them."[14] The whole world appears different because now the person can see the world as it really is: suffused with the glory of the God who made and redeems the world.

Although Edwards would disagree completely with Wordsworth's view of human existance, Wordsworth's fine Romantic lines in his "Ode: Intimations of Immortality from Recollections of Early Childhood" are early nineteenth century decendants of the insight Edwards' spoke of in his own recollections of conversion. Wordsworth wrote of his childhood:

> There was a time when meadow, grove, and stream,
> The earth and every common sight,
>   To me did seem
> Apparelled in celestial light
> The glory and freshness of a dream.[14a]

In the United States, the Transcendentalists represented the same kind of apprehension of the world. The Romantics and Transcendentalists were descendants of the Puritans in their desire to find God in nature. But the Puritans insisted that the God of Scripture revealed himself to the elect; the Romantics searched for a vague divine power suffused through all creation for those with the simplicity or aesthetic appreciation to find it. Edwards asserted that the vision of God was the result of the new nature; it was given by grace, not natural aptitude. He was a convenient source for such American Romantic Transcendentalists as Ralph Wado Emerson in his affirmation that the lowliest things could manifest God to the saints. Edwards wrote an entire book, Images and Shadows of Divine Things to show how God was manifested in everything from Scripture verses to flowers to bees. The divine glory was manifest in everything, for those who were enabled to see it by God.

According to Edwards, the vision of God given by the new sense was not, of course, for aesthetic satisfaction, even though by the nineteenth century many of whose who searched for it may have thought so. God's beauty was the beauty of holiness, and the new sense increased in the saints a growing sense of their own unworthiness

22

and God's great mercy in loving them. Edwards wrote of his own
experience:

> I felt an ardency of soul to be, what I know not
> otherwise how to express, emptied or annihilated,
> to lie in the dust, and to be full of Christ alone
> ... God in the communication of his Holy Spirit,
> has appeared as an infinite fountain of divine
> glory and sweetness;... pouring forth itself in
> sweet communication; like the sun in its glory.[15]

This was the kind of experience the seventy year old woman Edwards
wrote of had felt; this new sense was the consequence of the new
nature emplanted by the Holy Spirit. The new nature pulls the soul
towards God, so that all it sees, hears, thinks, and does relates
it to God. Having converted the person to himself, God pours his
love out on the saint, who now is enabled to grow closer and closer
to God. For Edwards, the agent of conversion and divine outpouring,
the key to the mystery of the election of God to man is the Holy
Spirit, the third person of the Trinity.

FOOTNOTES

[1] Edwards' "Personal Narrative," in <u>Works</u> (London: 1974) I, xiii.

[2] William W. Sweet, <u>The Story of Religion in America</u> (New York: Harper and Brothers, Pub., 1950) pp. 220-221.

[3] In <u>Select Works of Jonathan Edwards</u> (London: Banner of Truth Trust, 1965) v.I, p. 182.

[4] <u>Ibid</u>. p. 183.

[5] "The Manner of Seeking Salvation," <u>Works</u> (London: 1975) v. II, pp. 51-57.

[6] <u>Select Works of Jonathan Edwards</u>, v. I, p. 23.

[7] <u>Ibid</u>. p. 63-64.

[8] <u>Ibid</u>. pp. 31-33.

[9] <u>Works</u> (London: 1974) v. I, p. xii.

[10] <u>Select Works of Jonathan Edwards</u>, v. I, p. 36.

[11] <u>Ibid</u>. p. 41.

[12] <u>Ibid</u>. p. 44.

[13] John Smith, ed. (New Haven: Yale Univ. Press, 1959) pp. 206-7.

[14] <u>Ibid</u>. p. 264.

[14a] In <u>The Rinehart Book of Verse</u>, Allen Swallow, ed. (New York: Holt, Rinehart, and Winston, 1966) p. 185.

[15] "Personal Narrative," in <u>Works</u> (London: 1974) v. I, p. xlvii).

III: Grace: The Spirit in the Soul

> But when the Spirit, by his ordinary influences, bestows
> saving grace, he therefore imparts himself to the soul in
> his own holy nature....yea, grace is, as it were, the
> holy nature of the Spirit imparted to the soul.[1]

Most difficult and yet most central in Edwards' theology is
the person of the Holy Spirit, who himself, is God's saving grace
which transforms us into the children of God. Someone once remarked
that the villains in a story are much more interesting than the
heros. A modern poet has captured this characteristic of our nature
when he wrote of even little children;

> They'll go to sleep listening to the story of the
> little beggar maid who got to be queen by being kind
> to the bees and the birds,
>
> but they're all eyes and ears the minute they suspect
> a wolf or a giant is going to tear some poor woodcutter
> into quarters or thirds.[2]

So it is for us too, as I suspect it has always been for human
beings. Edwards himself, has suffered from this characteristic
of the great public. His great works on grace have been practically
unknown to Americans, but almost every high school student has read
his dramatic sermon "Sinners in the Hands of an Angry God", which
deals with hell fire and brimstone topics. But hard as we may find
it to be interested in and to try to understand goodness, Edwards
impells us to make the effort. Only if we can understand what
goodness is, that is, what is grace, will we be able to know the
fullness of God's action in us.

Is grace God's forgiveness, as the Reformers insisted? Is
it the ability to do good, as the Catholics claimed? Edwards
pressed further and lifted up an essential Biblical theme to
assert that the Holy Spirit himself is grace. In the souls of
the elect, the spirit dwells as a "principle of new life," that
is, he enables them to live a life pleasing to God. Besides
enabling us to do good, through the Holy Spirit, we have
communion with God, Father, Son, and Holy Spirit. It is, thus,
the Spirit dwelling in us, not some ability we ourselves have,
who is the source of all good for us in our actions, our
experience of God, and our hope for the future.

To truly apprehend the role of the Holy Spirit in the lives
of the saints, Edwards would first have us look at the state of
"natural man," that is, a graceless human being in this world.

25

Left to ourselves, we decendents of Adam and Eve are incapable
of doing good, because goodness is the work of one who is in
communion with God. Because our relationship with God has been
ruptured by sin, nothing we can do is worthy of Him. We live
in a condition of separation, like a husband and wife living
apart, but with much more distance between us. We react like
the children in the Nash poem, who find true goodness boring,
but find it exciting when someone hurts another or an individual
suffers misfortune. A glance at the headlines or the bestseller
list simply reaffirms this appraisal of our condition. As the
Apostle Paul so often reminds us, a pure and upright heart is
far removed from our capabilities.

Such a miserable state is ours, of course, because we, as
children of Adam and Eve, are separated from God by an unbridge-
able gap. We who are one moral person with Adam have lost God's
friendship and can do nothing to regain it. Grace, which is
just another word for God's love for us, cannot be earned, demanded, or expected from God. Original sin, which is a way of
speaking of this fundamental separation from God that each of
us is born into, prevents us from reaching God.

In the last chapter, we considered the movement the person
makes to reject his or her own sinfulness, the process of conversion. When the individual is moved by grace to accept Christ
as his or her Savior, the doors to divine friendship open. Or
seem to. As soon as one realizes that Christ is the sole
redeemer from our sins, one is confronted with a terrible new
problem. Christ lived 2,000 years ago (1700 for Edwards'
hearers) and I live today. How can the Savior, Jesus of Nazareth,
come to me if we are separated by time which I cannot bridge?

Thus, the state of the awakened Christian consciousness
would seem to be worse than that of the unconverted, who at
least are blissfully unaware that they are perched on the
edge of doom. The converting Christian knows that her or his
own sin needs a Savior, that I cannot heal my own soul, and
cannot bridge the time gap to find the Savior God has sent, Jesus
of Nazareth, the Christ. Is the state of this person now worse
than at first?

For Edwards, the solution to the dilemma is found in the
person of the Holy Spirit, who was given by Christ to the Church
to bring his salvation to all peoples in all times and places and
to transform the souls of all believers. Puritans, with their
roots firmly in the Calvinist tradition on this point, had always
insisted on the importance of the Holy Spirit, who "applied the
benefits of Christ's passion" to us. Acting on the soul, the
Holy Spirit changed the fallen soul into a holy one, able to
love and serve God and neighbor. But, Edwards adds what he

believed to be a new and crucially important element to Puritan
theology of the Holy Spirit and grace. In Edwards' view, not
only does the Holy Spirit act on the soul, but the Spirit dwells
in the soul and is itself the grace of salvation. Divine love
in the soul of the saints is the Holy Spirit himself, who becomes
the well-spring of activity and the divine life itself for us.[3]

Edwards assumed that the readers who were listening to his
arguments were familiar with the scripture passages which speak
of the Holy Spirit. In his Treatise on Grace, Observations on the
Trinity, Religious Affections, and other works which speak of the
Holy Spirit, Edwards frequently discussed Old and New Testament
references, which he regarded as crucial to his theology.[4]

Edwards was well aware of the Old Testament references to
the Spirit of God who brooded over creation (Genesis 1), and of
all the references to the Spirit as the breath of God giving life
and inspiring prophets. But his primary source for his theology
of the Holy Spirit in the soul was the New Testament. One might
well expect this, because only here did Jesus reveal the way in
which salvation might be given to each one.

In the Gospels, especially in Luke and John, the Holy Spirit
emerges clearly as the One who inspires and guides Jesus during
his life, and testifies to him as the Messiah (e.g. Luke 3:21-22,
4:1-21). Jesus gives the Holy Spirit to the Church as paraclete-
advocate and consoler (John 14:25-26, Acts 2:104), who will sustain and guide the body of Jesus' followers. In the Spirit, the
Christian is freed from the bonds of sin and death, and the Spirit
dwells in the Christian to give new life, and to make that person
the child of God. The Spirit is our communication with God (Romans
8). As ground and source of our unity in Christ, the Holy Spirit
welds us together as one, yet in such a way that each of us uses
our unique gifts and makes distinctive contributions to the life
of the whole. While this Spirit gives many gifts to believers,
the greatest of these is love (I Corinthians 13).

On this straightforward but solid base, Edwards constructed
a far-reaching theology of the Holy Spirit to explain how the
Spirit is grace and salvation to us. In order to do that, he
explores the relationship of the Holy Spirit to the Father and
the Son, and shows how, on the basis of this relationship, the
Holy Spirit gives us fellowship with God and one another. This
part of his teaching about the Holy Spirit is absolutely crucial
to our understanding of Edwards' theology. Edwards himself wrote
most about the Holy Spirit in theological works he did not have
time to revise and have published during his lifetime. But
although these works are difficult, for us to ignore them is to
be like the child who will only eat dessert, and refuses to eat
the meat and vegetables which give her the strength to live the

whole of her life, including dessert.

In his essay on The Trinity, Edwards identified the nature of the Holy Spirit, according to the scriptures. His primary idea is one which he received from the African Church father, Augustine of Hippo, through his Puritan forebearers. The Holy Spirit is the love of God personified, and any other notions about the Spirit must all spring from and return to this. In I John 4:8, Edwards notes that scripture clearly asserts that "God is love." But, Edwards continues, "in the context of which place I think it is plainly intimated to us that the Holy Spirit is that love." He connects this equation with the divine indwelling, noting that John says that if love dwells in us, God dwells in us, and then he notes that love is God's Spirit. Edwards insists that "God's dwelling in us and his love, or the love that he hath or exerciseth, being in us, are the same thing."[5] He weaves together two strands in John's thought, and insists that the indwelling Spirit of God is the divine love in us. Love is no mere abstraction or theological generalization, Edwards maintains, but the person of the Holy Spirit, who proceeds from the Father and the Son.

But how might one characterize this personal love of God which is the Holy Spirit? For Edwards, he is "pure act and perfect energy." God's holiness and love, he argues, are his perfect power and his power is perfect love. Edwards' use of this definition is based on his comparison with the human situation. When we meet a person and say of him or her: "What a marvelous disposition!" we are trying to express the basic energy which seems to inform everything which the person does. But when we speak of God, we are moved to identify as central the perfect love which is at the heart of all God's actions. This energy, which is absolute love, is the Spirit (Essay on the Trinity, 109-111).

God's energy, this Spirit-Love, is not simply God's self-directed love but is oriented towards self-giving. Giving life and beauty to all beings, the Holy Spirit is the harmonious form-giver of creation, who makes the world a living unity, in which all things cooperate. In the same way as God shares his beauty with all creation through the Spirit; love, joy, and eternal comfort, that is, the divine life itself, is given through God's Spirit. If God is truly Love, his fullness is not found only in his love of self, noble as that might be, but in the making of creatures to share his joy; and the establishment of his friendship with them. (Essay on the Trinity, 111-113).

Not only does the abstract doctrine of scripture and theology tell us about the nature of the Holy Spirit; Edwards asserts that all the scriptural images and emblems of the Spirit relate to the theme of love, peace, friendship: the dove, oil, water, fire, breath, wine, and so on. The message of all these material images

of divine things was exceedingly important for such an imagina-
tive Puritan as Edwards, who could see the whole drama of human
sinfulness before God in a winter evening's view of the stray
spider dangling over his fireplace. All the scriptural images
focused our minds on the Holy Spirit as God's Love, each image
illumining a slightly different aspect.

Having firmly established that the Holy Spirit is the personal
love of God himself given to us, Edwards asks us to probe further
into just what that means for us. In both his Treatise on Grace
and Essay on the Trinity, Edwards explores in more depth the ways
in which the Spirit relates to the Father and the Son, and thus
also draws us into divine friendship.

When he speaks of the relationship of the persons of the
Trinity to each other, Edwards uses the classical Western
orthodox terms. He could be quoting Augustine, Calvin, or any one
of his sixteenth or seventeenth century Puritan ancestors. God
the Father is the absolute, unoriginated God, "the deity in its
direct existence." The Son is God's perfect idea of himself, so
perfect that it exists as a person, while the Holy Spirit is
divine act, the divine energy poured forth in a perfect act of
self-love (Essay on the Trinity, 118). Although Edwards developed
those ideas at great length, for us two aspects are particularly
important.

First, Edwards regarded the divine fullness as perfect and
personal, but insisted that we gain a glimpse of God through the
created world and especially through ourselves. He had returned
to the words of Genesis, "let us make man in our image and likeness." If we are in God's image, then looking at our most noble
human characteristics can give us some idea of who God is. Of
course, we must always correct our understandings in light of
the biblical norm of Jesus as the perfect human. But we must
always take seriously the promise of God in scripture, and look
into ourselves to discover something about God.

Following Augustine, Edwards looks into the human spirit and
to it the acts of human consciousness. He asserts that we have
two primary activities and everything else we do or say or think
comes from these. We know and we love. Here is our human
analogue to the divine activity: ourself (God the Father) knows
(God the Son) and loves (God the Holy Spirit). In ourselves,
this is a very imperfect and fragmentary representation; in God
we see a perfect and personal Trinity of equals.

Second, the Trinity is a relationship of equals. Both of
these words are essential. The persons of the Trinity are not
three independent Gods stuck together like grapes in a bunch,
but are three interrelated aspects of one deity, each essential

29

and indispensable, something like three kinds of activity of one person. None could exist without the other, and to eliminate or add any would destroy the other. Each depends on the other for fullness, yet through sharing in the others, each is perfect God. None is superior; none inferior. The Father is not the Father without the Son, and both are united by the Spirit who is the perfect bond of love between them. God is truly God, only as the source and giver who knows and loves most perfectly; so perfect is the relationship that each are persons sharing in the others.

In talking about the role of the Spirit as the perfect love of God, uniting Father and Son, Edwards finds the connection between God and creatures. In his Treatise on Grace, Edwards says of the Holy Spirit:

"But the Spirit that proceeds from the Father and the Son is the bond of this union, as it is of all holy union between the Father and the Son, and between God and the creatures, and between the creatures among themselves." (64)

That is, because the Holy Spirit is the personal energy of love which joins the Father and Son in the unity of one Godhead, he can also be love who unites creatures to God and each other. The Spirit is thus the link who binds the saints to God. Because the Spirit is eternally active, eternally loving, he can always join humans to God, giving himself to those elected through Christ's passion and resurrection, without being bound by constraints of time or space. Through him, the eternal intentions of God for human history are actualized for us. The Holy Spirit is the Father's agent in history, to work his saving will in the world, spreading through history the saving work of the Son, particularly in the souls of the elect.

How can the Spirit accomplish such a mission? Edwards, again and again, phrased his response in words such as these: "I suppose that there is no other principle of grace in the soul than the very Holy Ghost dwelling in the soul and acting there as a vital principle" (Treatise on Grace, 74). A principle of action, in Edwards' language, was the source of power which enabled one to do or act in a certain way. For instance, a spider has a principle of locomotion which enables it to move about, weaving webs, trapping insects, and dangling over fireplaces. A person has a principle of life which enables him or her to move, think, decide for good or evil, and to act on that decision. In the souls of the elect, Edwards asserts, the Holy Spirit himself becomes the new animating principle.

Although Edwards doesn't employ it, a good word to use for

the Spirit's relation to the elect is the Latin word "subsume" or "take under". That means that the Holy Spirit "takes under" himself the whole human person, dwelling in the person to guide, need, guard, and bring the person to eternal life. Where before the principle of self-concern and self-preservation gave shape and meaning to one's life, when the Holy Spirit is in one's life, he uses one's self and all of one's gifts, abilities, and deeds to serve the Divine purpose. Now one is not "curved in upon oneself," but is a living temple of the Holy Spirit; "I" am not the source of my action, but it is the Holy Spirit within me. One's situation is like that of the Apostle Paul, who cried out: "Not now I live, but Christ lives in me."

With the Spirit dwelling in one, the person is not destroyed, but is given a new organizing principle, the divine life. Because a new life is animating the person, changes take place. As we explored in the last chapter, one has a new knowledge of God, a new sense of divine things. But this new sense, Edwards insists, is given to us only inasmuch as the Holy Spirit is within us. Furthermore, it is not given to us so we will feel heartwarmed and comforted (though indeed, this may be the by product of his action). Rather, we are enabled to have this new knowledge of God so that it may move us and change us. The Spirit doesn't want to modify something about us, but wants to transform our whole person.

"But all spiritual discoveries are transforming; and not only make an alteration of the present exercise, sensation, and frame of the soul; but such power and efficacy have they, that they make an alteration in the very nature of the soul." (Religious Affections, 340)

Edwards uses many different, imperfect images to give some idea of the intensity and extent of this change: We are like little suns which reflect the great sun, like mirrors in whom the divine light is reflected, like little foundations who receive their water from a great unending fountain flowing into them. All of the images try to give us a picture to represent our transformation.

When the Holy Spirit becomes the principle of our lives, giving us the capacity to know the divine truth, to choose it, and to act on it, he does not treat us like an automatic pencil or some other instrument to be used and discarded. Rather, as the Spirit acts in a person to transform him or her, the individual gradually becomes more and more like the God who dwells and acts within. Edwards' model for this transformation is personal. Thus, he conceives of the Spirit giving one knowledge so that one will see the absolute goodness of God and thus, want to be like him. So powerful and overwhelming is the divine truth, that if God is

31

truly within us, enabling us to see his goodness and love, our only possible response is to change and become more and more like this God so that we may love and know him increasingly well. All of the faculties of the soul are subject to the indwelling of the Spirit, Edwards insists (Religious Affections, 342). This aspect of the completeness of the Spirit's reign in the human heart would become exceedingly important to Edwards when he discusses the virtues which the Spirit establishes in us. At this point, we should simply note that Edwards insists on the absolute completeness of the reign of the Spirit in the human person. The Holy Spirit does not wish simply to alter our minds or our wills or our desires. The Spirit wants to change all of us. The indwelling of the Holy Spirit is an activity of personal integrity, in which God respects all of the human dimension of the person as being of equal importance in the relation to God.

Related to this notion is an emphasis on the goodness of all creation because we are created in the image and likeness of God; all parts of our human beingness are good. Thus, when the Holy Spirit dwells in us to transform us, all the aspects of our person are used because all of the person must be saved. The whole person is affirmed by God; no part is rejected or ignored. God takes us, warts and all, and changes us gradually in accordance with our own unique individuality.

Our transformation by the indwelling Spirit is, Edwards constantly reminds his hearers, a life-long process. He sometimes compares the presence of the Spirit in the soul to a seed, which must grow and flower over a period of time. In the Religious Affections, he states that "...a transformation of nature is continued and carried on by them (the transforming power and knowledge God gives) to the end of life; till it is brought to perfection in glory." (343) Just when Edwards has spoken great words of the power of the Holy Spirit and the soul, he reminds his readers that our progress is always incomplete and imperfect. The Spirit always acts in us, but our evil and self-centeredness always resist. Not all that proceeds from us is from the Holy Spirit. St. Paul who wrote that "Christ lives in me," also wrote "for I do not do the good I want, but the evil I do not want is what I do." Humility is the proper Christian attitude towards oneself and one's goodness. During our whole life we will experience this struggle and must be prepared for it. We are growing in grace, but have not yet been perfected in glory.

Above all else, we must remember that the Holy Spirit dwells within us not just to make us do good, or to restore us to the image of God which we lost through sin. All of this is given to us, in truth, but it is given to us because of the friendship or communion with God which the Holy Spirit brings to us. In his Treatise on Grace, Edwards simply asserts: "Our communion with God the Father and God the Son consists in our possessing of the Holy Ghost, which is their Spirit" (64). The elect are friends of God, having communion and fellowship with him in prayer, in glimpses of him in creation, in other humans, and themselves, sharing in God's eternal love, which is their joy and their happiness without end. Such is their lot, not because they deserve it, but because God graciously shares himself, his own love with them. The communion of God the Father with the Son is the Holy Spirit who becomes the friend of the saints, enabling them to be the friends of God. He who is the bond of union in the godhead is thus the communion between God and human beings, making the saints capable of eternal communion and joy with God. To be elected and called by God is to receive an eternal and unending communion with the God in whose image we are made and to whom we are growing increasingly closer, through the power of the Holy Spirit in a joy which has no end.

FOOTNOTES

[1] Jonathan Edwards. Charity and Its Fruits, Tryon Edwards, ed. (London: Banner of Truth Trust, 1969. Photolith reproduction of the 1852 edition) 36.

[2] From "Don't Cry, Darling, It's Blood Alright," in The Pocketbook of Ogden Nash, Introduction by Louis Untermeyer (New York: Pocketbooks, 1959) 73.

[3] Jonathan Edwards. Treatise on Grace and Other Posthumous Writings Including Observations on the Trinity. Paul Helm, editor (Cambridge: James Clarke and Company, Ltd., 1971) 69.

[4] For additional information about Edwards' use of the scriptures on this question, see his "Notes on the Bible" in Works of Jonathan Edwards, II 649-816.

[5] In Treatise on Grace, 108-109.

IV: Personal Change

"What do you think? A man had two sons; and he went
to the first and said, 'son, go and work in the vineyard
today.' And he answered, 'I will not go,' but afterwards
he repented and went. He went to the second and said
the same; and he answered, 'I go, sir,' but did not go.
Which of the two did the will of the father?" They said:
"The first." Jesus said to them, "truly I say to you,
the tax collectors and the harlots go into the kingdom
of God before you." Matthew 22:28-31.

Following in the footsteps of Jesus, Edwards tried to be a
good shepherd who knows his sheep. He knew that of all the pitfalls
of the earnest soul, perhaps the worst is self-delusion. Any
theology which claims that the grace of the redeemed is the Holy
Spirit dwelling within the believer runs a serious risk. No
problem could be more obvious. To be a temple of the Holy Spirit,
transformed increasingly into the divine likeness, is a high honor,
which one might think would make a person the envy of all,
possessing much authority within the Christian community. Alas,
some of the Christians Edwards knew through Great Awakening had
begun to act in just such an authoritative manner, claiming the
authority of the Holy Spirit for their actions, and asserting
their absolute demands on behalf of God.

For this reason, Edwards maintains that the Christian needs
a guide to tell him or her whether or not what the believer feels
to be the prompting of the Holy Spirit is in fact truly such. This
is the point of Jesus' parable. Not all who say: "I am the temple
of the Holy Spirit; I gratefully accept your grace, O Lord," are
Spirit-filled Christians. Rather, Edwards would claim, in the
spirit of Matthew's Gospel, that words and feelings, which may be
self-generated, are not proof of the love of God; but the deeds
which spring from an obedient heart are a surer guide.

After exploring just what grace in the soul is, Edwards then,
of course, had to speak about what results from this grace in
the soul. If the Spirit in the soul could be compared to a
principle of action or a seed, we must examine the flower which
bursts from the seed, the act which springs from the principle
of action. In order to have some reasonable notion of whether the
Spirit was dwelling in one's heart, or Satan or one's own pride
was deluding one, a person needed to look at the signs of the work
of God in a person.

In good Puritan fashion, Edwards spent much time asking what
were the signs of a true, as opposed to a feigned, conversion. But

35

we should also remember that he worked in the midst of the
Great Awakening, which, as we have seen, was a time when the
question "who is a true Christian?" was the topic of raging and
acrimonious controversy. Thus, everything Edwards said would
be weighed by opponents and proponents, and his words were thus
chosen with even greater than ordinary care. In addition,
Edwards was trying to avoid the error of previous Puritans, who
had compiled a virtual checklist for holiness. Edwards assumed
for himself the far more difficult task of designing flexible
yet demanding guidelines which respect individuality but also
attempt to "test" the Spirit.

In raising the question of what the life of grace looked like
in the life of one in whom the Spirit dwelt, Edwards does not
simply give a handy set of directions to follow. He is concerned
with the psychological process we must go through to be honest
with ourselves in asking whether or not we are responding to
grace or our own pride and self-serving. In a series of discourses
not published until 1788, Edwards explores this whole issue under
the title of "Christian Cautions; or, the Necessity of Self-
Examination."1

Edwards reminds us that in the Psalms, we are admonished to
pray "search me oh God, and know my heart; try me, and know my
thoughts...." To discern the authenticity of our Christian
experience, and our sense of the Holy Spirit's presence in us,
our feelings are not enough; rather we must emerse ourselves in
a life-long project of self-examination. Even the elect are not
free from this necessity, because they are in a process of
transformation by God. Much remains to be done, and we can find
it very easy and personally pleasing to fall back into sin.

"The heart of man is naturally prone to sin; the weight of
the soul is naturally that way, as the stone by its weight
tendeth downwards" (Christian Cautions, 175). It is very easy
for us, even with God's grace enfolding us, to yield to the
"natural man," who to a degree is within all of us. Did not the
Apostle Paul warn us of the good warring with the evil within us?
If even Paul felt the conflict, must we not also be cautious?
Edwards admonishes his flock of the sources of danger even for
those who might think themselves elect, and even be so regarded
by others.

Because our very nature is deceitful, because of our sin in
Adam, we must be very suspicious of our own impulses. "Doing what
comes naturally" may be the greatest and most self-deceptive
practice imaginable. And if we escape the danger of our own
blindness to our evil, Satan is ever-ready to work in us as the
"prince of darkness." Danger also surrounds us in the society of
other persons. We are inclined to yield to the force of custom,

Edwards cautions. Apparently the excuse that "we've always done that," is a venerable one.

Looking about for example from others can be equally deceptive. "Perhaps we see them [evil deeds] practiced by those of whom we have a high esteem, by our superiors, and those who are accounted wise men" (Christian Cautions, 176). Even then to say "everyone is doing it" expresses the powerful drive to find moral security in following the crowd, an urge which was as misleading then as now. But even if we resist all of these pitfalls, Edwards calls our attention to a far more subtle one. Most of us are morally short-sighted, he asserts. For instance, I am prone to spend much time in prayer and Bible reading, but disregard my obligation to love my family. I have, Edwards notes, failed to be aware of the full horizon of my moral obligations. Such omission can be at least as serious as any other form of self-deception, because through it we can twist and distort our whole moral selfhood.

How, then, ought one to behave in order to avoid moral stagnation, self-deceit, and the spiritual sickness and death which can result from a denial of God's grace? Edwards replies to this by listing several very practical aids to development. The first and primary method is to read the scriptures. In the Bible one learns what one must do in response to God's self-giving love. How can we know how to follow this rule of faith, unless we know what it is? "Everyone ought to strive to get knowledge in divine things, and to grow in such knowledge, to the end that he may know his duty, and know what God would have him to do" (Christian Cautions, 177).

But reading the Bible is not enough. Even when I am reading it, for instance, I must read it reflectively, always asking: What does this say to me? Most of us, the experienced Pastor Edwards notes, would do almost anything before we would admit the truth to ourselves.

"The generality rather think of others, how this or that person lives in a manner contrary to what is preached; so that there may be hundreds of things delivered in the preaching of the Word, which properly belong to them, and are well suited to their cases; yet it never so much as comes into their minds, that what is delivered   in any way concerns them" (Christian Cautions, 177).

No amount of spiritual discussion or holy reading will benefit us if we refuse to reflect, to see how the gospel is judging me and my inadequacy. Honest self-examination must be the beginning of spiritual awareness and free response to grace.

If peer pressure is important in influencing us to do wrong, the influence of good people can be equally significant in moving us to avoid evil. The best way to find out whether one's actual course of life is in accord with the scriptures, is to ask good persons. Perhaps one is not certain about what one ought to do, or is even lax in Christian action. If the person follows the advice of those practiced in Christian morality, he or she may be more sure of guidance from people who are probably very good judges.

Edwards then introduces a sobering but very specific suggestion: imagine yourself on your deathbed, and ask yourself if you will be proud of yourself when you think about this action which you are about to perform when you are about to die. Such a suggestion is an old one in the discipline of the Christian life, but a useful one. Often in the pressing concerns of daily business, we see our actions all out of proportion, and behave in light of immediate advantage or sudden fancy. Before you act, think, Edwards advises. As you are breathing your last, bequeathing the heritage of your deeds to those left behind, and about to step before God's judgment seat, will you be pleased with what you are about to do? You will be surprised, Edwards infers, with how your decision-making changes when you reflect upon it in light of your own death.

Listening to gossip is exceedingly wasteful of our time, but there is one sort of talk from others which we should hear and listen to well. What do others think of us and the ways we ought to improve ourselves? Of course, Edwards was aware of that most common of human characteristics - none of us wants to hear about our own faults, and especially not from others. Some of us, for instance, are very proud, but unaware of it. How can we find out about our problem? Someone must tell us, and we must humbly and politely listen. True friendship is a profound concern for the other, which involves speaking and hearing the painful truth, and then changing one's life in accord with what one learns. The path of Christian virtue is never a solo flight, but always a community enterprise.

We also ought to look at others' faults. Our motive ought not to be in order to criticize them, but because in seeing their failings we can take pains to correct the same in ourselves. When we observe any fault, anger, backbiting, pride, we should remember that the same can be found in us, and is at least as bad as in our neighbor. Therefore, instead of gossiping about our neighbor's flaws, we should take pains to eradicate the evil in our own lives.

In examining the lives of others, we are inclined to say, "so and so must know that we all can't stand the way she acts so

38

aggressive person to become suddenly demure and meek. What we must look for, however, is change and movement in the direction of significant improvement. We must never be content with the words "but that's the way I am." Grace demands more of us (Religious Affections, 357).

"Gracious affections," he then reminds us, "soften the heart, and are attended and followed with a Christian tenderness of spirit" (Religious Affections, 357). In Edwards' view, such tenderness of Spirit does not mean mushy sentimentality, or the hyper-sensitivity of the easily bruised ego, but the personal awareness of one who is engaged in an intimate relationship with God. All too often, Edwards avers, the great the danger is that a person who feels converted will go through all sorts of emotional turmoil, feel the impact of a "conversion experience," and then go back to his or her former ways, assuming that a converted person know longer needs to worry about behavior. They, as Edwards remarks, "instead of embracing Christ as their Savior from sin, they trust in him as the Savior of their sins." Grace is not, Edwards insists, merely a matter of feeling conversion and pro- fession of faith as a blanket approval from God which allows us to do whatever we want.

Rather, grace is the indwelling of the Holy Spirit in our souls, and his presence there should make us more aware of the obligations of our relationship to God. The saints are those who are aware of good and evil because they are sensitive to God in them. They are "like a burnt child that dreads the fire" (Religious Affections, 364). Having known how sin separates them from God, they will not readmit it to their lives, and they strive to be as godlike in behavior as they can. Such tenderness of conscience, Edwards affirms as the only proper attitude for one trying to respond to the Spirit.

Pointing out another aspect of the Christian character, Edwards described some of his flock:

"Some show a great affection to their neighbors, and pretend to be ravished with the company of the children of God broad; and at the same time are uncomfortable and churlish towards their wives and new relations at home, and are very negligent of relative duties." (Religious Affections, 368)

These people show what the saint ought not to be: dispropor- tionate in the practice of the Christian life. Because the saint's life is animated by the divine Spirit, and the "whole image of Christ" is being brought to fruition, "there is something of the same beautiful proportion in the image which is in the original.... there is symmetry and beauty in God's workmanship." (Religious Affections, 365)

superior to everyone. Why doesn't she change?" And we are astonished when we realize that she doesn't know how we feel, and doesn't seem inclined to change. Let us take heed, Edwards warns us. We too, are inclined to be blind to our weak spots. Let others' blindness keep us constantly alert for our own failures to see ourselves. Others' faults ought not to be fodder for attacks on them, but reminders to us of our own danger in disregarding our sins.

Edwards concluded his discourses on "Christian Cautions" by reminding readers of essential areas for self-examination in the life of an earnest Christian. In effect, he gives a Puritan group of sins which provide the material for a self-examination and confession before God. As such, it provides us with insight into the Puritan mind and Edwards' perception of his pastoral task, as well as the startling realization that the people of Northhampton who heard Edwards, and the other New Englanders who read him, were little different from us.

Before all else, Edwards reminds his flock of the crucial importance of perpetual prayer to God, and the necessity of common worship on the Lord's Day. He upbraids people for idle talk on the Sabbath, coming late to meeting, not singing, coming late to worship especially when it is cold, sleeping during sermons, and letting their minds wander from God to everything from dinner to serious sins like adultery or fraud.

Hidden sins are, of course, the most dangerous kind. Besides the wandering mind at worship, there are much more serious offenses. Edwards identifies two: the neglect of scripture which is essential for nourishing the Christian life; and the gratifying of lust, either in thought or deed. One's impression is that for Edwards' flock, these sins would be the most common and the most accessible. It might be very difficult for a poor farmer to swindle his clever neighbor out of several acres of land, but he could very happily plot adultery with the pretty servant girl in the wealthy landlord's house.

As one might expect, one's relations to the neighbor - or thoughts about them, or actions towards them, and our behavior in our families - form the longest sections of Edwards' admonitions. He reminds us of all the shady thoughts we harbor, our urges to defame our troublesome neighbor, our hopes of avoiding payment of debts, our attempts to ignore the wrong which we have done and are too proud to repair.

When we deal with others, in fact we often do not help our neighbor, either physically or spiritually. We enjoy destructive gossip, especially when we do it behind our neighbor's back. Add- ing to our other failures and many sins of the tongue, we are very eager to lie to others, or at least to hide the truth or stretch it a bit. Within the familes, besides general problems of dealing with others, we find special difficulties. Edwards was aware of the perenial type of "school (or work or church) angel, home devil." Many who shine in the outside world are despotic or destructive at home. While love should rule, anger and dissension in fact often reign. Husbands and wives are bitter and spiteful towards each other; husbands are over-bearing and wives rebellious. Neither children nor parents take seriously their obligations to each other. How contemporary this example sounds:

> "Parents sometimes weaken one another's hands in
> this work; one parent disapproving what the other
> doeth; one smiling upon a child, while the other
> frowns; one protecting while the other corrects.
> When things in a family are thus, children are like to
> be undone." (Christian Cautions, 183)

Edwards put many details in his sermons in order that his congregation and all his readers might have specific examples for their self-examination. The crucial and essential point was that the process of reflection take place in order that from the grace in our hearts might spring a true human response. Christian behavior is not a change mechanically worked, but a human transformation. Therefore, Christians must labor in cultivating the seed within, the flower of grace, which is unique for each.

Then having described the process of self-examination and the rooting out of sins, which is, after all, a very negative notion, Edwards also pictured for his people the positive image of a Christian, the ideal of the godly, grace-filled life for which we are seeking. In a Treatise Concerning Religious Affections, itself a development of three earlier works written during the heat of the Great Awakening,[2] Edwards explored the question. His construction of such a work rested on his basic faith, common to the Puritans, that the doctrines of predestination, conversion, justification, and sanctification, were intended for our comfort, not to leave us in a quivering mass of uncertainty. Much as the Puritans believed in self-examination, they equally believed it must serve a useful purpose. Not only must it keep you honest, but it must give you some idea of whether or not your religious experience is a genuine one.

As we have seen, one of the constant questions of the Puritan tradition was that asked of Peter on the first Pentecost: "What must I do to be saved?". If God is a truly loving and just God, he will not leave us in the dark as to whether or not we have received of his grace, or are just deluding ourselves. Furthermore, if the Holy Spirit in us is a principle of action, as Edwards asserted in his Treatise on Grace and Religious Affections,[3]

then there must be a correspondence between the principle and the actions. "As a being is, so it acts" was an axiom of class philosophy the Puritans firmly held to. Thus, by looking at on actions and personal characteristics as Edwards recommended, a person might have a reasonable assurance that he or she was not mistaken, that indeed the person was one of God's elect. By ga at the flower, one may have some understanding of the root from which it sprang.

So far in Edwards' work, we have only scrutinized his proc of self-examination and provided some negative examples. But h had a very clear idea of what the graced person would look like at least in terms of behavior. There were certain characterist manifestations of the Holy Spirit in the soul, which could be identified in order to determine the reality of God's transform agency. In Religious Affections, he outlined this portrait.

He identifies certain character traits which are present i the reborn Christian. One of the most notable is "the lamb-lik dove-like spirit and temper of Jesus Christ." (Religious Affec tions, 345) In a more abstract way, that means love, meekness quietness, forgiveness, and mercy. As we have seen, during the Great Awakening, one of the recurring problems for pastors and congregations was the insistence of those who claimed the prese of the Spirit, that they alone truly possessed grace, and they alone were able to judge between the saved and the reprobate. Such judgmental behavior was the immediate cause of serious cor flicts in the congregations, split many churches, and alienated many lay people and clergy from the ideals of the Awakening.

Edwards emphatically warned against this sort of behavior insisting that when we look at the figure of Jesus, we see an entirely different kind of life modeled for us. Christ spoke c himself as one "meek and humble of heart," and he condemned harshness. We who are his followers dare not espouse a differe ideal. In fact in the Gospels, Jesus even admonished his disciples to become as little children, the most unpretentious of persons.

Christian fortitude, then, does not lie in condemning othe and making "violent speeches" and complaining about the "intole wickedness of our opponents," but in living in humility and gen ness. Edwards was well aware that the harsh and condemning wor was often comforting to the one who uttered it, but in fact was a sign of spiritual weakness (Religious Affections, 351). We would do better, he asserts, to be forgiving, merciful, and ready to help rather than condemn, behaving as Christ did when he showed pity to others. As Edwards repeated in all of his descriptions of the change brought by conversion, we must of co make allowances for individual temperament, and not expect a hu

40

41

Edwards insists again and again that God's holiness is beautiful, in the most profound sense of that term. Thus, the godlike person will be beautiful and the virtues will be in proportion or harmony. He or she will be merciful to all, not just the ones the person likes. This mercy will be tempered by justice, so that all our obligations one to another are all upheld. A saint is joyful in delighting in God's mercy, but fearful of God's wrath, knowing all that he or she has done to deserve it. While one virtue may be stronger than another, none are lacking completely in the saint.

Some people, he warns, are very good at giving alms, but don't care about the fate of other peoples' souls. Others are very concerned about saving souls, but not bodies, because "in order to show mercy to men's bodies, they must part with money out of their pockets." (Religious Affections, 369) Both are equally short-sighted and lacking in virtue, for each fails to see that body and soul are both essential to the human being and by Christ's command, both must be ministered to with equal seriousness. And just as the true Christian will be concerned with body and soul of the neighbor, so too he or she will be more affected by his or her own sins than by other persons. The true saint is constant in intention towards others, not easily deflected by hurt from others. Some are religious in fits and starts, but they are not stable; the truly virtuous person exhibits a stable pattern of life.

In many ways, the notion of symmetry in virtue is central to Edwards' understanding of the way in which one discerns the godlike person, and the manner in which one can check up on one's own progress in bringing to fruit the grace within. The Holy Spirit within makes us into the image of God who is beauty and harmony, and thus we reflect this in our own personhood. Balance is the key to the living of the true Christian life. We find that symmetry is both the integration of virtues and the consistency and pursuit of the God-filled life.

In order to sustain this life of virtue, the saint is distinguished by an increase of the "spiritual appetite and longing of soul after spiritual attainments" (Religious Affections, 376). If one is serious about believing that grace is a personal relation to the Holy Spirit, then as one grows in this relationship, one's love must always increase. One who is not truly converted but only deceived by fleeting religious emotions, will not have such a personal love and desire to know God. The person's relationship to God will be so weak that he or she will simply not be capable of a sustaining a long-term love and practice of virtue. Enthusiasm soon dies when there are no roots to nourish it.

But besides being consistent, our desire must be for spiritual attainment, that is, for God. Many people are quite willing to put on the appearance of virtue, or holiness, so that others may esteem them, or in order to have others think well of them or even so that they themselves may think of themselves as holy and worthy of approval. The true saint, Edwards insists, is enamored of God, not of his or her own self-image. At this point too, we see Edwards, the pastor, with his experience of so many boastful people, proud of their own sense of the Spirit within. His caution to them is that the life of virtue is not one of public acclaim, but of constant practice, quietly unnoticed by others, calling no attention to itself.

"There is an inward turning of desire that a saint has after holiness, as natural to the new creature, as heat to the body" (Religious Affections, 382). Again and again, Edwards returns to the root causes of these various characteristics. If we are genuinely transformed with the Holy Spirit dwelling within us, then we do indeed thirst after holiness because our true self is holiness itself. The Holy Spirit is the center of our being, the focus of our personhood, and to seek holiness is to seek our true self in God. Conversely, not to have any great urge to holiness is a clear demonstration that the Holy Spirit is not in us, drawing us to himself. While the "natural man" is characterized by self-seeking, the graced person is earnestly in love with the God who dwells within and calls the person to himself.

Stated concisely, Edwards firmly insisted that "gracious and holy affections have their exercise and fruit in Christian practice." Our lives must be governed by Christian rules in all areas, and we must value this practice and make it our primary business in life, and persist in it to the end of our days. (Religious Affections, 385) Such rules of the Christian life are taught to us in scripture, both in terms of general characteristics, and also in some quite specific ways. Scripture especially insists on that element which Edwards frequently introduced into discussions of one or another aspect of the Christian life - constancy and perseverence. Time provides us with one of the surest indications of Christian character. It is practically certain that we can rest confident in God's grace in our soul if we can sustain the practice of the Christian life-style over a lifetime.

Edwards insisted quite emphatically that practice was the only demonstration one could use to answer the perpetually vexing Puritan question: "Am I following God's will?". On the basis of scripture, we can discover that practice is the proper proof of saving knowledge of God (e.g. Romans 1:21), of repentence (e.g. Matthew 3:8), of saving faith (e.g. James 2:22-24), of a saving belief in the truth (e.g. III John 3). In this matter of practice, Edwards was firmly in the Puritan camp, and thus, stood

against those who made feeling or a "religious experience" of the
Spirit's presence the norm of their religiousness. Saving faith
was saving because it was caused by the Spirit within, the source
of all good in us. That we are constantly practicing good is a
reasonably certain sign that indeed, the Spirit is functioning as
a principle of life within us. If no deeds are consistently
present, it raises questions about whether or not we might be
deluded. Just as when I looked at a flower pot, and see a
withered stem with a dried out blossom, and conclude that the
roots are dead, so too when I look at my life and see that my
good acts are few, far between, and very erratic, I may well
decide that the Holy Spirit is not within me. In fact, the
relationship between the indwelling Spirit in me and my Christian
practice is much more intimate than any human analogy may indi-
cate.

    Edwards takes this over-arching principle of the relationship
between Christian practice and grace, and shows how not only
religious principles of the virtuous life, such as we have already
examined, are essential, but also looks at specific kinds of good
practice. He asserts that Christian practice is the surest
evidence which we can have that we have indeed left the world and
come to Christ and that we love and trust Christ. Our behavior
should show our love and humility, our fear of God, thankfulness,
earnestness, hope, joy, fortitude. All of these specific virtues
must in fact, be present, because they are all specific and
necessary ways of manifesting the beauty and symmetry which must
be in the Christian because they are in the God who dwells in the
Christian and makes that person new in Christ.

    We should be encouraged to note one significant difference in
Edwards' moral theology from his Puritan forebears. Rather than
laying down laws and rules of conduct, Edwards prefers to teach by
saying what ought to be in our souls (such as joy, and giving some
examples of things we ought not to do, and others which we ought
to strive after.) When all is said and done, he is overwhelmingly
positive and loathe to lay down detailed and comprehensive lists
of Christian practices. His rules are guidelines and examples,
rather than all-encompassing codes. He takes this position because he believes that grace is the person of the Holy Spirit
acting within us, and that our moral behavior is the manifestation
of profound personal relationship with God. Thus, what we
primarily need are positive statements and examples which aid us
in removing the debris of our sinful and selfish urges in order
that the Spirit may transform us more easily and fully into the
image of God.

    Within the context of his exhortation to Christian practice,
Edwards warns of the two great dangers which threaten the earnest
Christian of his time (and, one might add, are very much present

today). The first is, that spiritual experience is the "main evidence of true grace" (Religious Affections, 451). Obviously on the basis of Edwards' analysis, to assume this would be a great mistake, because true grace, experience, and practice, form an essential and unbreakable union. If the Spirit is truly in one, then the person will have a sense of divine presence, but the grace will also manifest itself in the good deeds which are its natural product. If the Holy Spirit truly is present, then under its transforming influence, we will begin to behave in a Christ-like way. In and of itself what we feel to be religious can be very misleading, as we have seen, and it can be equally deluding to urge people to have a religious experience of any one particular kind. Put in a contemporary context, a revivalistic attempt to make people "feel the presence of God" is false. If the Spirit is present, the divine power will make itself felt. To urge anyone to speak in tongues, and to insist that if, and only if one can do so, is one a good Christian, is equally false. If I do so, I become the arbiter of my own religious feelings, and I make my favorite feeling, the foundation of my Christian life. Rather, it is Christian practice rising from a life in which grace is experienced which is the sure sign of a divine presence.

Second, to conclude the Religious Affections, Edwards warns against those who regard any attempt to discuss specific practices of the Christian life as sheer legalism. We might call these people the "as the Spirit moves me" party. To say that grace alone matters and that no one can say what the promptings of God will ask of us is, Edwards firmly insists, to thoroughly misunderstand the biblical message. In fact, the scriptures place a great deal of weight on the practice of virtue, and not to see virtue and good practice as necessary and observable aspects of biblical religion is to totally misunderstand the meaning of faith in Christ.

In no way, Edwards adds, dare anyone try to usurp God's prerogative and say who must do what in a certain way in order to be saved. We must give careful attention to the uniqueness of each person and each situation. No one of us dare ever sit as final judge over the other, for that would be proudly to take the place of God. At the same time, we must follow Christ, and "lay the stress of the judgment of ourselves there, where he has directed us" (Religious Affections, 460). That is, in the scriptures Christ has given us a means whereby we can apply some judgment to ourselves. The signs of grace he has given us are guideposts on our pilgrimage, not clubs to beat over the heads of other people. What Edwards has tried to do is no more than to apply the biblical message to the question of the correspondence between our behavior, our religious feelings, and the grace of God which redeems us.

FOOTNOTES

[1] _The Works of Jonathan Edwards_, Dwight and Hickman, II, 173-185.

[2] Earlier works which contributed to _Religious Affections_ were:

A Faithful Narrative of the Surprising Work of God in the Conversion of Many Hundred Souls in Northampton (1737);

The Distinguishing Marks of A Work of the Spirit of God (1741);

Some Thoughts Concerning the Present Revival of Religion in New England (1742).

[3] Eg. _Treatise on Grace_, 32; _Religious Affections_, 340-344.

> For a time he avoided taking any part in it; and his
> own temporal comfort, and the welfare of his family,
> seemed to require that he should persevere in the
> same course. But his conscience forbade it.[1]

Virtue is not simply for the benefit of an individual or
family, according to Edwards. In his view, the universe was
created to be an harmonious whole, with God as its source and
goal, and all things working together to please and praise him.
Because God has made us to be part of a whole, our ethics have to
be concerned with our place in the whole. We cannot act for
self-centered reasons, or to please those whom we love, but must
make our actions benefit the whole. The right ethical question to
ask is: How does my decision effect the interrelationship of God
and the universe and myself? The Holy Spirit is the very power
of God bringing all things into harmony with Him. If the Spirit
is in me, I will act in accord with the Spirit's unity creating
power.

All of Edwards comments about ethics must be seen within
this framework of his, which asserted that everything was created
for one purpose, to serve God's glory. All creation is a unified whole in God. Thus, no matter how intense our individual
relationships with God may be we must all actualize our true place
as parts of the whole. In his work Dissertation on the Nature
of True Virtue, Edwards notes that: "God is not only infinitely
greater and more excellent than any other being, but He is the
head of the universal system of existence...."[2]

Therefore, even though we have spent a great deal of time
dealing with the manifestations of the Spirit in the individual,
and with a person's behavior towards family and friends, we must
also ask how Edwards moved his theology of the Holy Spirit's
influence even further, into the social dimension. He insisted
that we must examine our actions to see how well they fit into
God's purpose for the world and our role in this activity.
Furthermore, we must act so that God's greater purposes are
achieved. The Spirit within us is not only the Holy Spirit of a
personal relation to God, but also the Spirit of a universal
harmony between God and the creation, which urges us on to do
God's will.

Such language is, admittedly, very abstract. We can easily
comprehend what individual change might mean in Edwards' theology,
but it is much harder to imagine how Edwards would think of a
more social or universal ethical demand. We have good reason to

suspect that if he had lived longer Edwards' works would have given us the kinds of examples of social ethics that he does when he speaks of personal conversion and personal ethical behavior. The fact remains, however, that he did not. So to gain some insight into Edwards ethics for the human community, let us turn to an illustration from his own life to see how he thought responsible people ought to behave in society.

In the eighteenth century, as is also true today, white settlers had serious ethical difficulties trying to decide how to treat the Indian population. On the one hand, the whites regarded the land as rightfully theirs because they worked it and made it productive in a way the Indians had not and did not want to. They shared a history in which the Indians were driven further and further into the background. On the other hand, all of them recognized that the Indians were present, and had to be dealt with by peaceful means or by force. Many of the whites were also convinced that the Indians were human beings who only lacked education to make them just as good as the whites. The Great Awakening added a dimension of urgency for seeking the conversion of the Indians, in order that they too might share in the outpouring of the Spirit.

In December of 1750, Edwards was called by the white congregation at Stockbridge to be its pastor and at about the same time was offered a post as Indian Missionary to the Housatonnuk Indians.[3] He walked into a controversy over Indian rights which would occupy him for the next three years, until 1754. Consuming as this conflict was, it provided a situation in which he was able to act upon his theories of Christian Social Ethics.

An Indian Mission at Stockbridge had been established in 1735 and shortly thereafter a school was established, financed by the Boston Commissioners of the "Society in London for Propagating the Gospel in New England, and the Parts Adjacent." Timothy Woodbridge was its first instructor, and he tried to teach the Indian children and counter the pernicious influence of the white settlers. Stockbridge itself had been settled by whites in the 1730's, allegedly to protect Indian Treaty rights and to trade goods with the Housatonnuks. All was not as the legistature, which had given the settlers privileges and grants of land, had hoped. Woodbridge suspected some settlers of cheating and the Indians and he knew that they sold the Indians "large quantities of ardent spirits," thus undercutting all the missionaries efforts to do any good among the Housatonnuks.

In 1739, Rev. Sergeant, the missionary to the Housatonnuks, tried to establish a boarding school for the Indian children, in order that they might live at the school and have access to books

and more extensive practice in the English language than they
would have had if they had stayed at home. He also hoped to
rescue the Indian children from the dangers of the alcoholism
which was so prevalent among their own people. Rev. Isaac Hollis,
a mission minded pastor near London, generously agreed to pay
for the room and board for the Indian students, and the cost of
their instruction. Mr. Sergeant hired as temporary help a local
retired soldier, Captain Kellogg (who was illiterate!) and a Mrs.
Ashley, who spoke Iroquois, and her husband Captain Ashley. In
1744 the French War broke up the school, and in order to keep
receiving Hollis' money, Kellogg kidnapped some of the Indian
boys and took them back to his home in Connecticut.

After things had calmed down, Rev. Sergeant received an
offer of some land from the Housatonnuks, and acceptance of an
offer to send their children and students to his school from a
number of the Mohawks. So he began to construct a boarding school
for the Mohawks. But whom do you think he hired? Captain
Kellogg, who was coming out of hiding from Connecticut. Mr.
Sergeant must have been very desperate, insensitive to the Indians,
or just inordantly trusting. Happily for the Indians, about the
same time, the fortunes of Woodbridge's Housatonnuk school began
to rise and he employed a young Housatonnuk named John Wonwanon-
pequunownt as an assistant.

Thus, when Edwards arrived on the scene there were two
Indian schools competing for funds: Woodbridge's, which was
founded through the Society in London for Propogating the Gospel
in New England in order that the Housatonnuks might be educated,
and Kellogg's supplied through Rev. Hollis' generosity and used
by the Mohawks. One was well run, whereas Kellogg's was at best
inadequate, and the Indian boys were often forced to work on
Kellogg's farm. The development which was to create much dis-
turbance for Edward's in his time at Stockbridge was Kellogg's
desire to get more money for his school and raise additional funds
for a girls' school which his relatives, the Ashleys, would be
in charge of. To almost everyone on the scene, it was clear that
Kellogg and his associates had no interest in the Indians, but
wanted to pocket the money for themselves. In the first years
after his arrival, Edwards took it upon himself to battle Kellogg
and his associates in an increasingly bitter struggle to protect
the Indians and wrest control of his school from Kellogg.

Just before he assumed his duel post at Stockbridge, Edwards
wrote to Rev. Hollis, giving him a discrete warning of some of
the problems at the Indian school, and outlining some of Edwards
own theory of education. Edwards criticized Kellogg's method of
teaching because the children did not learn the meaning of the
English language in which they were being taught. He explained
that the Indian children, who did not know English, were not taught

50

to understand the language, but only to recognize certain words. Thus, when they were instructed in reading, they only apprehended sounds, and could never grasp the meaning of the words they were reading. Because of all of this further education was cut off from the Indians. The sad consequence was that because the Indians never learned to understand the meanings of the words which were used to educate them all the missionaries' endeavor was of "little effect for benefit."

As Edwards explains to Hollis, knowing the language is the key to access to European culture and religion. To this end, Edwards proposed that either English children should be brought in to learn with the Indian children, or that the Indian children live with the whites for long periods. He preferred that the Indian children live with whites, as that would be more effective, if only the Indian parents would give their consent. Because the instructional task was so vital, Edwards insisted on the necessity of the highest quality instruction for the Indian schools. (Works I cxxiv)

By summer of 1751, after Edwards had assumed his charges in Stockbridge, the Mohawks as well as the Housatonnucks were increasingly ready to send their children to school, and were also highly receptive to the missionaries' preaching. Edwards wrote to the Speaker of the Massachusetts Assembly in order to influence that body to keep its treaty obligations to the Indians and to actively defend their rights. He strongly believed that "if the utmost good faith was not kept with the Mohawks the whole plan of instructing them would be defeated...." (Works I cxxxv). This would not be the last time Edwards would involve himself in a public political stance in order to save his Indian Mission.

A number of other English lay and clergy were interested in supporting the Indian Mission school, and wrote to Edwards for advice. Such correspondence gave Edwards an opportunity to voice some of his concerns about Kellogg's school as well as to elaborate on some of his educational theory. He continually underlines the necessity of aiding each child in understanding what he or she is saying and reading, in both secular and religious learning. Besides the catechism, Edwards suggests that children (and he is thinking especially of the Indian students) should learn history, geography, and spelling. Both boys and girls should receive this education, and Edwards urges the importance of either bringing English children to the Indian school, or preferably arranging for Indian students to live for a time with the English. (Works Vol. I cxxxvi - cxxxix).

Happily for Edwards' designs for the education of the Mohawks, in February of 1752, the Rev. Gideon Hawley arrived, appointed by the Boston Commissioners to teach the Mohawk children (thereby replacing Captain Kellogg) and to do some preaching to the Mohawks and other Iroquois. Hawley's arrival lent urgency to Edwards' request to the Boston Commissioners to appoint some local impartial trustees for the Indian schools. In addition to a substantial increase in the number of Indians coming to the Mission schools, a significant rise in the amount of donations to those same schools was occasioned by the progress of the presently existing Housatonnuck school and reports of Indian receptivity to education. Edwards had kept his eye on the Ashleys and Captain Kellogg for some time, and was very fearful of what might happen to the money if they or their friends got ahold of it. At this point, alas, all hell began to break loose. An enemy of Woodbridge's (the good teacher of the Housatonnucks) and his nephew got themselves appointed to the Board of Commissioners in Boston for the Mohawk school. They managed to have the London directors recommend Mrs. Ashley as the teacher for the Mohawk girl school, and set up one of the family to be local director of Indian Affairs. By these appointments they also hoped to divert the funds that Hollis and his acquaintances were sending from England for the Indians in order to benefit themselves.

Edwards' was positively horrified. He had never trusted the Kellogg-Ashley group, and now his worse fears were being realized. The tale of the next two years in Edwards life in Stockbridge is one mass of anxious maneuvers and counter moves by Edwards, who stood almost alone for the Indians, and the Kelloggs and Ashleys, who sought to gain full control of the Indian school money, which they regarded as the biggest windfall of their lives.

Edwards spent a considerable amount of his time during 1752 writing impassioned letters to the Commissioners in Boston, trying to clean up the situation. He was quite alarmed for the future of the school because the Mohawks knew they were being used and deeply resented it. Over half left the Stockbridge area. Edwards was roused to action, because he feared the end of all his hopes for educating and converting the Indians.

The Kellogg-Ashley faction became more bold. One of their friends, visiting the school, struck one of the Indian children on the head with his cane. Of course the Indians were furious, but Hawley could do nothing. Finally the Indians went to Edwards, who managed to convince the offender to pay damages. The Kellogg-Ashley crowd was angry at this affront to them, showing no concern for the Indians, and plotted to get rid of Edwards. They resorted to all sorts of tactics during the next month, ranging from trying to buy up the town to force Edwards and Hawley out, to pressuring the Boston Commissioners to get rid of Edwards and Hawley.

Having failed to get rid of Hawley or Edwards, their opponents attacked Edwards before the Massachusetts Assembly. The Assembly and Boston Commissioners reaffirmed their faith in Edwards, who had written to some of them about the affair. In the meantime the Mohawk school had been burnt down, and everyone suspected the Kellogg-Ashley group of arson. If they could not have the present school, the Kelloggs and the Ashleys certainly thought they should be able to get money for building new schools in place of the ones which had so tragically burnt down.

While the Indians were very fond of Edwards and Hawley, and appreciative of their efforts, they were so disgusted with the political machanations and disturbances in the school that most of them finally moved from Stockbridge to their former lands. When in February of 1754, Edwards was finally given full control of the Mohawk and Iroquois schools by Mr. Hollis, very few of the Indians remained. Hawley had already moved away in disgust, and finally the Stockbridge school was combined with Hawley's school at nearby Onohquaqga. As Sereno Dwight, Edwards' first biographer, notes, if Edwards had had control of the school in 1750, at the beginning of the Indian influx, unquestionably the school and missionary endeavor would have been a significant success (Works I, clxiii). Edwards fought valiantly, but his victory came too late. The French and Indian War, which began in 1756, gave the death knell to Edwards' hopes for the Indian Mission.

What can we learn from this painful and lengthy controversy in which Edwards was involved for the welfare of the Indian schools? We should remember, first of all, that Edwards was not embarking upon this struggle because he was a bored country pastor, looking for something to interfere in. He had chosen the post at Stockbridge, and stayed there despite offers of pulpits in Scotland and in Virginia. He could have left if he had chosen to. Furthermore, this was an intellectually very busy period in Edwards life. Besides working on phamplets to counteract his detractors from his controversy in Northampton, he was also engaged in writing his monumental Freedom of the Will. He did not need a lengthy and at times rather acrimonious struggle to divert him, particularly since he was still weary from his struggles at Northampton. Nonetheless, the arguments over the Indian Mission and school contained the substance of Edwards' ethical beliefs.

When Edwards wrote to his London correspondence, he underlined again and again the importance of aiding the Indian children to understand their lessons so that they could have access to culture and the Christian religion. While we may feel quite uncomfortable with Edwards' assumption of European cultural superiority, we must remember that he was an eighteenth century American, not one from the twentieth century. He wanted to give the Indians access to an education which would give them full knowledge of the Bible, and freedom to share in the culture of the whole world which Edwards knew, not just the limited one of the Indians. Underlying his effort was his assumption that whites and Indians were

53

part of the human community, and neither were inherently inferior to the other.

From Edwards' theological perspective, there was no question that all human beings were equal in God's sight, and ought to be given an equal opportunity to know God and respond to His Spirit. Such equality was not merely in "religious" matters, but ought to pervade every aspect of human life. Until all of God's benefits, economic and cultural as well as religious, were open to all, God's words of promise were not made fully real. Edwards thus was internally impelled to struggle for the Indians as much as he was able. He continued his interest and personal commitment even after he had won his battle at the school, sending his second son to dwell for a time at the Indian boarding school at Onohuagga so that he might learn the Iroquois language.

In keeping with his belief that Indians and the white settlers were inherently equal in human capabilities, was his underlying assumption that virtue and the love of God are the only true measures of personal work. Thus he fought the whites, his cultural equals and his parishoners, in order to defend the rights of the Indians, most of whom were barbarians in his eyes, and had for the most part not yet been converted. Human value was to be measured in terms of service of God and neighbor, and in that respect Edwards judged his white peers harshly and stood at the side of the Indians who gave him their loyalty in return.

If we could put into a few words what seems to have been Edwards' guiding principle, it might be something like this: The good of the whole human community, joined in one purpose of service to God, must be served above all else. Edwards never asked himself if he would make enemies, nor if he was looking out for his family and himself, and being differential to the people who could make his life comfortable and get him a good job. Whether the Indians were powerful or weak was unimportant to him. All that mattered was that Edwards served the good purpose of God's whole human creation, made to love and praise him, even though such service brought no benefit but only trouble to himself.

We should thus not be surprised that in 1755, only one year after he had finished his controversy over the Indian schools, Edwards wrote his great ethical work, Dissertation on the Nature of True Virtue. In it he explored more theoretically some of the ethical ideals he had exercised in his earlier controversy. In order to understand what true virtue is, one must note that Edwards links it to "benevolence to being in general." (Nature of True Virtue, 3).

By benevolence Edwards does not intend that vaguely warm feeling we sometimes have, or the perfunctory donation of time or money to a worthy cause. Benevolence is a "willing of good" which involves a whole-hearted commitment of the person to do good. No fainthearted goodwill is Edwards' ideal, but a total self-giving which demands that person and deeds be dedicated to good.

"Being in general" is the object of our willing, according to Edwards. For him this means not one or two creatures, or even God alone, but rather being in general is God and each and every creature as it relates to each other and to God as the head of all. All creation unites in glorifying the God who made it, in serving Him and fulfilling His will. When any part fails to do so, it is out of harmony with God and all other beings; that is, it is in sin. Virtue is our willingness to be in unity with God and the universe which serves Him. It is our desire to serve God in all things, rather than to put ourselves at the center of the universe.

Lest Edwards' definition sound as though he has visions of our being harnessed in a painful and severe service of a merciless God, Edwards reminds us that this service of God involves love. We know that God is beautiful, that goodness and perfection are found in Him, and that all His deeds are expressive of His goodness and holiness. Creation's beauty comes from its attachment to God and its harmony with His goodness. If we believe this, and if we truly see the beauty of God and the world as it fulfills His purpose, how can one not love it? What could be more attractive to us than the harmony of creation with God and what more repugnant and ugly than a break in this harmony, appearing to disfigure the joyful unity?

How, then, can we do other than love virtue? True virtue, one may say, is a love for God and all things in relation to Him. From this love, all our individual acts spring (Nature of True Virtue, 5). We see the "big picture" first, Edwards seems to tell us, perceiving God as the center and all things focused on Him. Within that perspective we can then make decisions about how we should act in specific situations, because we have grasped something of the vision of how things ought to be. All our individual actions have meaning and purpose, we may also conclude, because we have seen the whole. If we have not, we are apt to get side tracked and make false or at least inadequate decisions.

All beauty in the world, Edwards notes, is "but the reflection of the diffused beings of that beams who hath an infinite fullness of brightness and glory "(Nature of True Virtue, 14-15). God indeed is "head of the universal system of existence... whose being and beauty are, as it were, the sum and comprehension of all existence and excellence: Much more than the sun is the fountain and summary comprehension of all the light and brightness of the day. (Nature of True Virtue, 15)." All things depend on God, derive from Him, and find their meaning from Him. He is universal being, because everything is oriented towards Him and serves His purpose. Virtue can thus be most succinctly termed the love of God, because when we speak of God we necessarily include everything, in as much as everything comes from and is intended towards God.

Most of us, if we are honest, have to admit that we do not make our life's decision on the basis of any such view of the world. Our choices of taking or leaving a job, purchasing a house, going on a journey, or any other ordinary event, are based on our own self-interest. We are really not concerned with God's plan for the good of the world, or even for the welfare of our immediate neighbors. Normally, our decision making process begins and ends with us, with some necessary attention to our closest family members, a bit of consultation with our friends, and an eye open for any social or legal consequences. (Nature of True Virtue, 45 and following).

Put most bluntly, most of us are madly in love with ourselves. We may tell ourselves that we are only thinking of our children's welfare (or husband's, or wive's), but when the thin veneer of self sacrifice is scraped away, we find ourselves staring our ego squarely in the face. Honest scrutiny reveals to us that we respond differently to objects and events which benefit others from those which reap benefits for us. Our enthusiasm, consistency, concern, all are influenced by the degree to which things profit us. Honesty compels us to admit that we are much more quick to help others if they will later help us, or if our charity will make us look good to other people. It is much more difficult to fight for others, as Edwards did for the Indian Mission, if we know that our jobs and security are on the line.

When we are trying to think of what virtue ought to be, our self love triumphs again. If a poor person is asked to describe goodness, he or she is most apt to describe a very generous person. A small child will name an adult who readily dispenses all the toys, candy, and treats a child could desire. An adult will list the characteristics of the one who most benefits him or her. Who would begin by asking what ought one to do for the good of all of us under God? None. We want virtue to be that which most profits us.

As if our own selfishness were not enough of a problem as we try to come to an appreciation of true virtue, we must also reckon with the negative effects of social pressure, especially education. All of us are influenced by the prodings and promptings of others, the rumors, and the subtle pressures. But the most basic moral attitudes are instilled in us through our education as children. If we doubt this truth, Edwards invites us to look at people of another culture. All humans are the same at birth. What makes us so different in our moral attitudes? Education. (Nature of True Virtue, 60) We can see why Edwards was so insistent on proper education for the Indian children, but also why he demanded a good religious education for his whole flock. He himself saw to the thorough education, moral and intellectual, of all his children, boys and girls. Childhood patterns predominate, he knew, and dispose us towards true or false virtue with an influence unmatched by any force other than the Holy Spirit himself.

In short, we will do almost anything to avoid facing the truth about ourselves and the world: We are all creatures of God, to whom we owe our primary allegiance, and according to whose will we ought to structure our relations with one another. God is not the first one we consider, but the last, if He even enters into our consideration at all. But let us suppose, unlikely as it might be, that we would consider God in our moral deliberations. What might happen then?

It is entirely possible, Edwards suggests, that we might come to realize the importance of God's role in the moral universe. After all, if we think about the matter, we must immediately recognize that God is the creator of all and the one to whom we owe supreme regard. If you present me with a beautiful scheme, showing my obligations to God and to everyone else, I will immediately agree about my duty towards God and obligation to others. The fly in the ointment is that I don't act on the basis of abstract knowledge.

Show me all the philosophy and theology you will, but rational argument alone does not move me to action. I must believe, I must be convinced that my actions ought to be carried out with regards to God's intentions. Just to tell me that I should do something will have no effect at all on me. I must see the world, and my self in relation to that world, in such a way that I will act in accordance with God's will. Natural desires tend towards myself, and are of no help. I cannot, Edwards concludes, give myself the compelling vision, the "new sense" that puts my actions in harmony with God.

Use of the term "spiritual sense" (Nature of True Virtue, 102) alerts us immediately to Edwards' intention of underlining a point he had introduced before. Conversion and a new heart, a new nature, must proceed and give rise to God centered action. True virtue, in Edwards' scheme, is not simply a conscience telling me to do good, for that would have no sustained or lasting affect. Rather, true virtue is love moving me to action. Love is no other than the Holy Spirit, and we are brought again to the core of all of Edwards' theology. The Spirit working in us is the agent of conversion and of all our good. Just as in the area of personal

change, so also in social ethics, the Holy Spirit alone can bring
us to the rebirth which is the beginning of all good and harmonious action.

Taking into account our conversion to true virtue through the
power of the Holy Spirit, what ought we to do in our ordinary lives
to bring ourselves into harmony with God's desire for the whole?
To begin, I must first keep in mind the full consequences of my
actions, or at least try to act in perspective of the whole. For
instance, even though I may always want to decide what I shall give
to the church on the basis of how much spare change I have at the
end of the week, what would happen if everyone who is a church
member gave on that principle? Why am I giving, out of guilt or
because I want to aid God's work in the world? If I love God and
want to forward God's loving work in the world, why am I giving
God spare change? How can I call myself a Christian if God is so
low on my priority list? One with a "new sense" would see the
world as desperately in need of the church's work, and give accord-
ingly. This is only one small example, but what would happen if
we all started to make our decisons this way? Such a world would
indeed be much more in accord with God's own beauty and harmony.

But not only we as individuals, but our family, social, and
community groups must begin to shape our actions in accord with
God's intentions. One of Edwards' great griefs with his community
at Stockbridge was its failure to rally to the needs of the Indians.
What would have happened if the inhabitants of Stockbridge had
persevered in aiding the Housatonnucks and the Mohawks? How
would the history of our nation and that of Christian missionary
work have been different if the white community had been more
responsive to Indian needs? What does this say to us, who are
often so remiss in attending to the needs of minorities and the
powerless among us? How can God's world be in harmony if our
communities deliberately (or even unthinkingly) repress some of
their inhabitants?

Let us not restrict the application of the ethical demands
of God's love to individuals and small communities. Edwards was
equally insistent that nations also must tend to God's command
for full harmony with Him and with each other. This involves
a very honest examination of national policy. Edwards has very
harsh words for nations who cloak their selfish designs under a
mantale of righteousness:

> So a nation that prosecutes an ambitious design of
> universal empire, by subduing other nations with fire
> and sword, may affix terms that signify the highest
> degree of virtue, to the conduct of such as show the
> most engaged, stable, resolute spirit in this affair,
> and do most of this bloody work. (Nature of True Virtue,
> 107).

We can easily delude ourselves into believing that our love for more money and land is really our desire to spread our culture and religion to the savages, whom we must therefore conquer. Edwards opposed such opinions in his own lifetime, and we can be sure he would oppose them today.

His view of national responsibility for the good of all people has particular poignancy for us today, in a time of global communication. We are indeed responsible for one another. The United States Government does have a responsibility for human rights in the Soviet Union, and Saudi Arabia must be concerned for India's grinding poverty. No nation dare care only for itself; that is the greatest and most dreadful glorification of self love. Edwards admonishes us that in God's eyes we are all brothers and sisters, nations as well as individuals. Christians must take up the burden of moving governments to behave as those responsible for one another, not mere slaves to national self interest.

We are all members of one another, Edwards reminds us, all children of God. If we remember that God is our head, and let the Spirit of God enter our hearts and transform us according to His will, we can live a life of true virtue, in love and harmony with God. Not only are we our brothers and sisters' keepers, we are all responsible for the whole world as God wills it to be. We ought not to be irrationally optimistic in our expectations of what we can do. Most of us will find out, as Edwards did at Stockbridge, that our achievements will be short-range and limited in time and effect. But on the other hand we can never lose sight of our goal, that it is God who is our head and gives us life and in whose life we strive to bring our universe into harmony. Our lives must be dedicated to doing God's will, to acting out the prayer we pray to God daily: "Thy kingdom come, thy will be done."

FOOTNOTES

[1] Dwight and Hickman, Works I, clvi.

[2] William K. Frankena, Editor (Ann Arbor, Michigan: University of Michigan Press, 1960) 15.

[3] I am calling the Native Americans "Indians," when tribal designations are not used, because this was the language Edwards employed.

God thus appears gloriously above all evil; and
triumphing over all his enemies, was the great thing
that God intended by the work of redemption, and the
work by which this was to be done, God immediately
went about as soon as men fell; and so goes on until
He fully accomplishes it in the end of the world.[1]

How does America's existence and behavior affect the rest of
the world? Most of us would respond in terms of economics,
military power, or diplomatic influence. For Edwards, the answer
could only emerge from a consideration of God's purpose for the
world and His gifts to and challenges for America. What for us
would be a purely secular question, concerned with supply and
demand and national alliances, was for Edwards a matter of
eternal importance before God.

History is not a popular study in schools today, but for
Edwards and his Puritan predecessors, it was an area of intensive
investigation. God acted in history, they believed, and if you
carefully examined the history of the world, from creation until
now, you could discern the purposes of God, the intentions of
God being acted out on the stage of history. God's will for the
world could be known primarily from the scriptures, but also from
nature, and a good Puritan also read the will of God in the actions
of nations and of individuals in them.

Redemption was God's primary purpose when He made the world.
God made the world to love Him and to share His life with Him, to
praise God's glory eternally. God, therefore, did not let the
forces of sin in human beings thwart His purpose of love. The
whole of history is a testimony of the way in which God works
out His intention of redemption among human beings. Edwards
writes:

God thus appears gloriously above all evil; and
triumphing over all his enemies, was one great thing
that God intended by the work of redemption; and
the work by which this was to be done, God
immediately went about as soon as man fell; and
so goes on until He fully accomplishes it in the
end of the world. (History of Redemption, 23)

Creation of the world had an end, Edwards firmly believed, but not
simply in the sense of the calendar ending, as though one might
say, "The world will end in two thousand A.D." Of course the
world would have a final time in history, but Edwards was thinking

of something far more profound than a chronological termination.
Creation had a goal (Telos, in Greek), to glorify God, and
God's intention was to direct everything in the world towards
that end. Thus, history can only be properly understood as the
expression of God's glorious intention of redemption in human
time and space. We can only properly interpret history if we
see everything which occurs as having meaning as part of God's
saving activity.

Edwards identifies God's purpose in the story of redemption
as including several elements which can be perceived in the annals
of the human race. God's goodness is sovereign over all, and
is manifest in all His works. Nothing which occurs is evil or
malicious in intent. God is not the cruel deity of some pagan cults,
nor the indifferent observer who occasionally is referred to in
modern novels or philosophies akin to the Deism of Edwards' contemporaries. All that happens in the world is directed by God's
providential care, and if we are able to grasp the whole picture,
or significant parts of it, we will begin to understand that God
directs each individual event to the good of the whole.

Once human beings have fallen, it would seem that Adam,
having been given free choice and ruined his opportunity,
would have destroyed human relationships to God. At this point,
God could, one might think, either have ignored us, or simply
selected out of the world those whom he had chosen with
absolutely no concern for the force of human history. But God
did not choose to separate His grace from the course of the world.
Therefore God has determined that history will be the story of
the salvation of the world and the leading of human beings to
follow God's will. One may not, in Edwards' scheme of things,
speak of a "salvation history" distinct from secular history.
All history is the history of redemption.

God intended to bring all the elect into unity with Christ
who is the head. In this way all creation, which is made for the
elect, can find its unity in God. Thus, one may also speak of
history as the account of the preparation for and the gathering
together of rational creation to make up the body of Christ.

Creation's story is also the recounting of the glory of God
manifest in the activity of rational beings. In the elect, the
mercy of God is perfected and His image in them is fulfilled, as
they praise and glorify Him. The reprobate, who are damned by God,
also have a place, because they show the just judgments of a God
who is worthy of praise and glory. All of these rational beings
living and working together manifest the various dimensions of God's
glory as expressed in a finite creation.

God's glory is displayed in the work of redemption itself. The

Father's glory is in creating, sustaining, and designing the redemption of the world. Through the Son the work of redemption is carried out in the incarnation, life, death, and resurrection of Jesus Christ. The Spirit works redemption in the church and brings the world to a service of God. All history must then properly be perceived by us as a glorification of each person of the trinity, who are united in essence and in one purpose of redemption, with each sharing in the work of salvation. (History of Redemption), 22-25).

History, in Edwards' mind, was no mere optional study, but a way of perceiving the plan of God, His glory, and something of His nature. So crucial did Edwards consider history to be that he intended to write a history of the world which would be so ordered as to show forth the theological truths of God's inter- action with us. In 1757, when the trustees of Princeton College were trying to convince Edwards to become president of that institution, he enthusiastically wrote them about a new kind of theology which he was experimenting with, "a great work..., a body of divinity in an entirely new method." The History of Redemption is the skeleton of his endeavor, which was to take account of all the events of history, beginning "from all eternity" and continuing to the last judgment. Edwards described his method:

> [It] appears to me the most beautiful and entertaining,
> wherein every divine doctrine would appear to the
> greatest advantage, in the brightest light, in the
> most striking manner, showing the admirable con-
> texture and harmony of the whole."[2]

In his attempt to use history as a basis for his theological method, Edwards certainly represents a new development in theology. But his notion that the history of the world is a basis for a Christian understanding of God and His work has deep roots in theology. Those roots helped to form Edwards, and also have had a very direct influence on the American consciousness as a whole. Before looking at Edwards' understanding of the way theology emerges through history, let us take a brief look at his intellec- tual ancestors. They insisted that theology could not be only inward directed, nor ought it to stop with the Bible, or even with the history of our church, but had to encompass the whole of human history if it expected to speak of the glorious works of God.

We can only understand American Puritanism if we can find its roots in England, for American Puritanism is both child and sibling of its English counterpart. For English Puritans the events of history were of crucial importance, and we can discern the source for this preoccupation deep in English religion. At least as far back as the first stirrings of the Reformation, an idea was present in English religious thought which we might call "Deuteronomical theology."[3] This Deuteronomical theology derives its name from the theology undergirding certain historical books of the Hebrew Bible: Joshua, Judges, First and Second Samuel, First and Second Kings. The Deuteronomist author understood the action of God as manifesting itself through the events of Israel's history.

When disaster struck Israel, the Deuteronomist wrote about it as God's judgment upon the people for not keeping their covenant with him. Prosperity was God's blessing upon Israel for obeying his will, and a sign that people had "returned to the Lord." Eventually such a view would be expanded in the Book of Isaiah to an affirmation of God's universal Lordship over history. No event of history was random or haphazard; everything meant something and was directed by God for His immediate purpose. As the Puritans (and their English predecessors) adapted this view, they in no way interfered with God's gracious election or reprobation of individuals. God alone gave or withheld salvation regardless of human endeavor. In history, however, God directed events but also allowed us human beings to respond to or reject his will. Our salvation was determined by God's election, but the material welfare and historical fortunes of a nation in its political, social, and religious spheres, depended upon its obedience to the covenant. Disobedience resulted in God's punishment. Only by renewed obedience to the covenant law could prosperity be gained.

The reformer William Tyndale in the 1530's wrote of England as a new Israel in his preface to the Book of Jonah. He began by assuring that beginning with Israel all the nations of the world had been called to repentance. Starting in the misty dawn of English history with Gildas, he related all the crucial events in England's history to God's call to repentance through his messengers, the people's refusal to hear, and finally their judgment by God. He claimed that the reformation was a crucial time for England, in which God called the people to obey his law faithfully, and be his true chosen people. If England reformed herself according to God's word, Tyndale believed, then she would realize her covenant as the chosen one of God.[4]

English Puritans accepted Tyndale's analysis as their own, and viewed England as God's chosen nation, the new Israel, and themselves as God's instruments to guide the nation into a right observance of her objectives before God. When the Puritans (and Pilgrims, who differed little from them), came to establish the new Israel over here, they hoped that as the reform became strong over here it would spread to England. Our history books did us a disservice when they talked about Puritans coming to New England to find religious freedom. Never would it have crossed a good Puritan's mind to think about religious freedom. They sought to bring about God's kingdom on earth. In order to do that, they needed a community where everyone, elect and reprobate alike, obeyed God's covenant will. Thus there was no freedom, for everyone had to obey the law. If everyone obeyed the law, the new Israel would be effected by God and he would establish His dwelling on earth, beginning with them. Even those laws which we call blue laws, they would have claimed were necessary for the perfect observance of God's law. In God's chosen land the believer and the ungodly alike had to obey even the smallest restriction and to subscribe to the highest public moral principles.

In 1630, when the Puritans came to Massachusetts Bay Colony, their leader John Winthrop made very clear to his fellow settlers, Puritans and others, what the Colony was to be. Against the background of a lengthy discussion of the ideal body politic, Winthrop notes the distinguishing characteristic of the Bay Colony. He warned the settlers that they have entered into a covenant agreement with God, which should be approached as seriously as any other legal agreement, and of course even more so. Having given us a "special commission," God expects us to strictly observe His will in "every article." Because we have entered into a covenant with Him, we must observe it well and be rewarded, or disobey and experience God's wrath.

Using the covenant affirmation in Deuteronomy chapter 30 as a base, Winthrop promised the settlers that if they obeyed God's call to keep His word, then:

> ...the Lord will be our God and delight to dwell
> among us, as His own people, and will command a
> blessing upon us in all our ways, ...when ten of
> us shall be able to resist a thousand of our
> enemies, when He shall make us a praise and a
> glory that men shall say of succeeding planta-
> tions: the Lord make it like that of New England:
> for we must consider that we shall be as a city
> upon a hill....

In concluding, Winthrop warns the people that as a settlement set apart, on a hill for all to see, they had to model proper human response to God's word. If they obeyed, all people would praise God because of them, but if they failed, before all the world they would be condemned and destroyed.[5]

By 1662 a new generation of New Englanders colonized the land, and a growing number questioned the value of the religious fervor of the founders of the colony. Although many remained faithful to the original ideals of the founders, an increasing number were more and more involved in the profit and loss possibilities of New England's economy. In the light of such declining morale among the congregations, is it any wonder that the clergy spent much of their private time and public opportunities in the pulpit lamenting the infidelity of their flocks?

In the first chapter, I reported about the jeremiads, sermons of lamentation which the ministers preached to exhort the people to repent and return to New England's mission. One of the most effective of these preachers seldom took to the pulpit, but wrote one of New England's most read poems, "Day of Doom." Besides writing about the judgment day, Michael Wigglesworth also interpreted contemporary events in the light of New England's covenant vocation. In 1662, he penned "God's Controversy with New England," a lengthy (438 lines) lament for New England's punishment by God with an extensive drought.

To resume the whole work would be tedious, but Wigglesworth does provide us, as he does about judgment day, with a poetic compendeum of New England popular belief. He begins his dirge on the drought with an image of America before the colonization as "a waste and howling wilderness." He then proceeds with an account of the settlement of New England and God's covenant with the people, through which they were protected. He lists temporal and spiritual belssings at great length, and then morns over the "lukewarmness" of the present generation, who have not kept up the vigorous service of God observed by the first settlers. Within this context, he then speaks of the drought, ill health and increase in malaria and fevers, as the punishments of a God provoked by the ill behavior of the New Englanders. If and only if they repent, will God respond to them in love and cry out, "still in New England shall be my delight."[6]

Not only in Wigglesworth's exceedingly popular verses but even among later Puritans do we find the same deuteronomic theology which inspired the earliest Puritans. As late as 1690 the great Boston minister Cotton Mather delivered an election sermon (given on the days when civil elections for governor and magestrates were held) on Nehemiah 5 verse 19 in which he proposed the same sort of theology. He asserted, "you may see an Israel in America!" New England was specially chosen to be "a plantation for the Christian and Protestant religion." He warned that his listeners political as well as spiritual happiness (this was, after all, an election sermon) depended on their covenant obedience to God's word. If they obeyed His words, remembering their errand to this land, they would prosper, but disobedience would mean God's rejection and their decline.[7] Unhappily, as we saw in the first chapter, very few people paid any serious attention to the ministers' cries about New England's obedience to the covenant. By Edwards' time, the deuteronomic theology no longer animated New England's religious consciousness.

But if one did not accept the old view of America's place

as the new Israel, how could one apprehend the nation's mission?
Did it have one; was it to become a nation without a soul?
Edwards highly valued history, and America's special place in it,
but he tried to give it a new interpretation which moved in a
quite different direction from his Puritan ancestors'. Whereas
the earlier Puritans had emphasized human response and obedience
to God's will, he spoke of the whole process of history as the
work of the Holy Spirit. Both actions and reactions, success and
failure in history, were due to the direct activity of God's Holy
Spirit. Thus he was able to correlate all the important works of
God, the gracious salvation and transformation by grace, individual
and corporate ethical response, and the nation's role in history,
as the Holy Spirit's work.

As we have seen, Edwards insists that God controls every
aspect of creation and the world's history for His glory and our
salvation. Everything which occurs works together as a unified
whole for this purpose, guided by the Holy Spirit. Edwards used
a variety of images to express the movement of history, guided by
the Holy Spirit. He wrote of a fountain which poured forth its
life, never diminishing, but all of its water issuing forth from
the same beauty. Sometimes he compared history to the light shining
forth from the sun, which all reflected the glory of the same
sun. On occasion he wrote of history as being like a great machine
which has one end, and in which all the parts cooperate to one
purpose (History of Redemption, 17).

If we can view all the events of history in their proper
perspective, we would see them all cooperating together like
the parts of God's chariot we read of in Ezekiel's vision:

> The wheels of providence are not turned round by
> blind chance, but they are full of eyes round about,
> as Ezekiel represents, and they are guided by the
> Spirit of God; where the Spirit goes, they go: And
> all of God's work of providence through all ages meet
> in one at last, as so many minds meeting in one center.
> (History of Redemption, 350)

All the works of God, which cooperate in harmony, are like the
wheels of the chariot which operate together as the vehicle of God.
Each of the events of human history is the work of the Spirit. The
Holy Spirit is source of action and unifier, who draws all in to
God's good purpose of salvation.

Edwards' view of the work of the Spirit in directing history
leads him to assume a different opinion about the role of religious
obedience and America's role in history than one might have expected
from a Puritan. While the seventeenth century Puritan exhorted
his congregation to repent and follow God's law so that the nation

67

might be blessed and God be praised, Edwards did not do so. In effect, he did not believe that we were free to accept or reject God's commands. Rather the Holy Spirit moved us to obey God's law, or withheld from us the grace of obedience. Even the sermon was a servant of God's activity, which did not really move people to do something which lay solely within their own power. The Holy Spirit was the only power, all else were his servants, carrying out His will.

When Edwards tried to interpret the meaning of the Great Awakening in the 1730's, he explained it as a manifestation of God's grace poured out upon New England. Thus, we can immediately see an example of his shift in emphasis from human obedience to God's commands to God's grace which produces human obedience and response. While earlier Puritan ministers had explained strengthened dedication after a period of moral decline as stemming from the people's renewed covenant loyalty to God, Edwards accounted for the "outpouring of the Spirit" with an improved moral conduct of the people as totally due to divine action and purpose in history. Edwards' own hopes for the revival of religion were not that the nation might be more prosperous because God's law was being obeyed, or even primarily that individuals would be saved, but that:

> This glorious outpouring of the Spirit of God over
> the greater community was a sign that God was draw-
> ing the world closer and closer to Himself for a final
> consummation of this life and a closer union in glory.
> (History of Redemption, 290, 302-307).

We should note two aspects of Edwards' belief about the activity of the Holy Spirit. The first is that the Spirit alone is the mover who causes all events to happen. The second is that the Spirit is moving the whole world - quickly, Edwards thought - towards its final consummation. While the Puritans had expected the earthly kingdom of God which would being in the heavenly kingdom to be initiated by its own covenant obedience to God, in Edwards' scheme only the work of the Spirit will initiate the earthly kingdom. In order to understand how Edwards expected the consummation of the world to come, we must examine more precisely what he thought America's role in that consummation of the world would be.

Edwards considered the discovery and settlement of America, which he thought would usher in the final items, to be a crucial event, just as had Winthrop, Wigglesworth, Mather, and other Puritans. But Edwards tried to interpret the whole of the American history as an expression of the Spirit's activity. America he called "the principal nation of the Reformation" (History of Redemption, 282) because it was the last nation of

the Reform faith to be established, and would, he hoped, be purer
than the tainted continental nations.

So intensely did he insist that the Spirit's activity must
be anticipated above all else, that he even repudiated some of the
instrumental causes which the Puritan divines themselves had
indicated would help to bring in the coming of God's final triumph.
Not even learning, so highly prised by the Puritans, could bring
in God's kingdom. We could only pray that,

> ...when the appointed time comes for that glorious
> outpouring of the Spirit of God, when he will him-
> self by his own immediate influence enlighten men's
> minds; then may we hope that God will make use of
> the great increase of learning as a means of the
> glorious advancement of the kingdom of His Son.
> (History of Redemption, 290).

Such great work can be carried out only by the Holy Spirit, not by
any human effort. One might read here implicitly a criticism of
the Puritans who gave such a great role to the human effort to
morality and to education. Edwards was in favor of high standards
of both morality and education, but he would maintain that only
God's Holy Spirit, who indeed is the final source of both proper
learning and morality, can bring about God's Kingdom. We must
be exceedingly humble about those instruments which we use in God's
service. We must always remember that the Holy Spirit is the only
true actor and we are only the receivers.

America's discovery and settlement he regarded as the beginning
of the establishment of God's kingdom through the work of divine
providence. When God chose, Edwards asserted, the Gospel would
have "glorious success" and all the natives of America and people
at the fartherest ends of the globe would receive the Gospel. Even
the mariners' compass, he suggested, must have been a work of
providence because it would enable missionaries to sail to distant
places to convert the heathen. (History of Redemption, 284).

The role of America within this scheme is not primarily to do
something but to receive the work of the Spirit. Edwards expected
that God would extend His saving activity, already active in New
England, throughout America:

> Then shall the vast continent of America, which now
> in so great a part of it is covered with barbarous
> ignorance and cruelty, be everywhere covered with
> glorious gospel light and Christian love; and instead
> of worshipping the devil, as they do now, they shall
> serve God, and praises shall be sung everywhere to
> the Lord Jesus Christ, the blessed savior of the
> world. (History of Redemption, 314).

America's role is to receive the Holy Spirit and respond to it. The work is thus not America's, but God's. As the receiver of God's grace, America can be a vehicle to others, can praise God's glory and testify of Him to others, and thus manifest to them God's glory. America cannot do anything to change the world, as the Puritans thought it could, but it can be the servant of God's Spirit.

When the Holy Spirit has chosen to transform America fully, and not merely give it the foretaste we have experienced up to this time, we may happily consider that this will be a major part of God's preparation for the establishing of his kingdom. At that time Satan's kingdom will be overthrown, and Christ's kingdom will be perfectly established in the world. (History of Redemption, 284, 315). It will be a time of light and knowledge, holiness and piety, peace and love, the triumph of the true church, the greatest spiritual and temporal prosperity and great rejoicing. (History of Redemption, 319-328). It will be, in short, the time of the perfect triumph of the Spirit, when the work of the Spirit is brought to perfect fruition.

Within this context of history as the work of God's Spirit, what remains of the Puritan vision of America as the new Israel? If you think that America's role depends on her own choice, and is the result of her obedience to God's law, the response of Edwards theology won't be very consoling. No nation is essential for God's purpose, whether it be an old or new Israel, old or new England. God's will shall be accomplished through the work of his Spirit, and does not depend on our responses. America's activity does not cause the temporal or spiritual success of God's cause; the Holy Spirit moves us as he chooses according to his design. Thus, no nation is an absolute, or necessary to God's work. Edwards certainly had high hopes for what might have been achieved toward the establishing of God's kingdom, but when they failed and the Great Awakening petered out he would not have fallen into doubt about the nation's mission as did so many of his English and American Puritan contemporaries. He would simply have assumed that the Spirit had his own purposes and laws, acting according to his own plan. He would have retained his faith that God's plan would triumph, regardless of what appeared to us. God was merely adding another act to the drama.

Thus we see that both Edwards and the Puritans agreed that America was a principal agent of the Reformation, and that the mission of America was (or ought to have been) the beginning of the establishment of God's kingdom on earth. The two differed, however, with respect to a couple of significant areas. Whereas the Puritans insisted that human response and effort do play some part in the establishing of God's kingdom, Edwards denied it. Both individual salvation and national convenants were direct works of the Holy Spirit, not generally dependent on our decisions.

Besides emphasizing the agency of the Spirit, Edwards correspondingly reinterpreted America's status with respect to God's kingdom. As the Puritans regarded their own role, it was easy for them to laud themselves as God's chosen ones, at least partly because of their own virtuous reponse to God. Their constant temptation was to see themselves as an example of what we can all be if we would only follow God's law. Edwards eliminated all opportunity for self-congratulations, and proposed for America what we might call a servant role. All we do individually or collectively is directly the work of the Holy Spirit, so how can we take any credit for it? Even pride in the excellence of one's service is inappropriate, and the highest goal is to be so absorbed in God one forgets one's ego and is totally at God's service. For Edwards, this ideal is as valid for a nation as for an individual.

How did those who followed Edwards, both those who read him and those who ignored him, respond to his accentuating the Holy Spirit as a mover of history, and America as God's very humble servant? Not very well. Even Edwards' most enthusiastic admirers seemed to have ignored this dimension of his message. The evangelicals of the late 18th and 19th centuries, many of whom expressed profound admiration for Edwards' teaching, insisted that America was delegated by God to Christianize the world. Important as their work was, they tended to regard their own interpretation of the Gospel as normative for everyone, and their own endeavors as virtually indispensable to God's mission. God was indeed at the center of their concerns, but they highly exalted their own efforts to be American Christians responsible for the world.

Similiar counterparts to the evangelicals can be discerned in the secular world. These are the Americans whom later historians called the proponents of "manifest destiny." They believed that it was the United States'mission from God to rule its land from shore to shore (thus the Mexican-American War and Indian battles were good for us and approved by God), and to guard the world, spreading American Christian culture to benighted heathen everywhere, either by persuasion or by force. They personified a secular version of the evangelical stress on American efforts to convert the world. These people wanted to conquer because it was America's mission to be supreme.

Both the evangelicals and the more worldly dominating Americans would have benefitted highly from serious attention to Edwards. His History of Redemption was often read but seldom heeded. They ignored his theology of the Holy Spirit and made America into God's representative who established the house rules for the world. Both groups believed that America was called to glory, spiritual or

worldly, and preferably the two of them together. In Edwards'
scheme of things, we are all called to a repentance and service
which themselves are God's grace given to us. God's alone is the
glory; ours the service, to be carried out as God wills. Edwards'
theology of the Holy Spirit suffused a profound aura of humility
into his appreciation of America's role in history. One can only
lament that his thought was not taken more seriously. Our own
history might have been spared many painful sins and errors if
we had only paid attention to him.

FOOTNOTES

[1] Jonathan Edwards, The History of Redemption, 23.

[2] Works, Dwight and Hickman, I, clxxiv-v.

[3] The term has been applied and analyzed by James Spalding, "Sermons Before Parliament (1640-1649) as a Public Puritan Diary," Church History, XXXVI, 1 (March, 1967) 3-14. It derives, of course, from modern Biblical criticism and is applied here in a derivative way.

[4] William Tyndale, "Preface to Jonah," Doctrinal Treatises and Introductions to Different Portions of the Holy Scripture, Walter, Parker Society, XLII, 452-459.

[5] John Winthrop, "Model of Christian Charity," in Edmund Morgan, Puritan Political Ideas, 1558-1794 (Indianapolis: Bobs - Merrill Co., Inc., 1965) 76-93.

[6] Michael Wigglesworth, "God's Controversy With New England," in Seventeenth Century American Poetry, Harrison Meserole, editor (New York: New York University Press, 1968) 42-54.

[7] Cotton Mather, "The People of God" in Morgan, Puritan Political Ideas, 233-349.

Epilogue

Where does Edwards' greatness lie? We must remember that we have considered only a small quantity of the work that he has written. Even so, we can appreciate his theological insight and pastoral discernment. Given the variety of conflicting religious claims and experiences competing for recognition as the truth, he was able to identify the Biblical insight which was most central to the needs of his situation, and to construct a theology which would illuminate it.

If we see here some resemblance to our own times, I think that we shall not be mistaken. American Christianity is the possessor of a variety of positions within, ranging from the fundamentalist Biblical literalists to unitarian humanists, and all the shades in between. After some hesitation, it is increasingly apparent that the charismatic renewal movement is settling in to be a permanent part of the religious scene, and often laying claim to be the authentic form of religious experience. At the moment, an inward turned, sometimes conservative style of religion is the fashion, but who can tell how long the changing winds of popular demand will blow in that direction?

Many call "Lord, lord," but they do not do so with one voice, and often they do not even have in mind the same lord. Where shall the honest Christian turn? Edwards provides a perspective from which one can begin to sort out some answers. Religion is not to be equated with morality, or experiences, or even knowledge of the Scriptures. The Holy Spirit is the one who comes to us to make the Scriptures speak to us, to dwell in our hearts to give us communion with God and fellowship and responsibility with one another. Edwards does not give us all the answers, but he provides us with a "guide for the perplexed." If we listen to his advice, we will be somewhat less inclined to gambol off after every religious fad, and be more prepared to follow steadfastly the one who claimed to be the Truth.

When we take Edwards' seriously, we also find him a bit of a spur for those Christians who wish to be born-again in the Spirit and then to revel in God's love for them. We are never saved for our own benefit, Edwards reminds us. God saves us for his own glory, and the "praise of his glory" requires us to work without ceasing for the material and spiritual welfare of all peoples, whether we like and agree with them or not. God's is the glory; ours is an unceasing service impelled by a communion of love with the God who wills good for all his children.

But what of those who labor for good causes in the name of

74

God and the church, but have no personal sense that God is any more real than the Jolly Green Giant? To them too Edwards extends a warning, insisting that religion is not simply working for good causes. After all, we can work for justice and the good of others because we fear revolution and want to head it off, or because we need other people to depend on us and think of us as noble, or for any one of hundreds of somewhat doubtful motives. As good as our work may be, let us not call it religious, when it springs from our own selfish purposes.

True religion must be founded on a personal relation with God which is the gift of grace, the Holy Spirit dwelling in our hearts. As a fruit of this relationship we serve others, because they too are creatures of God, worthy of our service. We are not chosen to set ourselves above others, but to serve humbly, walking according to the truth God has given us.

In these bicentennial times, when we are trying to discern what we have done as Americans, and where we should go as a nation, Edwards provides a very helpful prospect as we seek to know ourselves better. He was an American born and bred, who reflected on his own experience in a new land, providing the insight of one who lived on the edges of the European settlement. At a time when many were somewhat undecided about what America ought to be, he outlined a vision of America as a servant of God's glory in the world. America's hope would be built not on what she could do to other nations, or even to herself, but on what she would let God do in her. Such a relationship would be the foundation of her great place in the world. An American theologian, Edwards combined a theologian's comprehensive grasp of the relationship of all creation to God, with an American's endeavor to help his nation grasp its interrelationships to other peoples.

In brief, Edwards is for us the exemplar of a profound and substantial theology. He has set before us the lineaments of a relationship to God which is a genuine mystery, more lasting and unfathomable than any other personal interconnection. To confess that the Spirit of God is acting in the whole of the universe, our history, in others, and perhaps even within ourselves is the beginning of faith. To acknowledge the Spirit of God, moving us and vivifying the image of God in which we are created, can be a searing and life-transforming experience. It requires us to put God at the center of our lives and our expectations. Edwards' theology demands that we turn our lives inside out, and respond to the promptings of perfect love, the Spirit of God. His is a challenge which is not to be relegated to the eighteenth century, but is equally compelling to us in the twentieth.

Selected Bibliography

Works of Edwards

The two best of the 19th century editions of Edwards' works are:

Works. E. Williams and E. Parsons, ed. 8 vol. Leeds: 1806-1811.

Works. S. Austin, ed. 8 vol. Worcester: 1808.

The only complete edition of Edwards' works presently in print:

Works. E. Hickman, ed. 2 vol. London: 1833. Reprinted by the Banner of Truth Trust, London: 1974.

The critical edition presently being produced is that which began under Perry Miller's editorship from the Yale University press: New Haven, 1957 and following:

Freedom of the Will, Paul Ramsey, ed., 1954.
Religious Affections, John Smith, ed. 1959.
Original Sin, Clyde Holbrook, ed., 1970.
The Great Awakening, C. C. Goen, ed., 1972.
Apocalyptic Writings, Stephen Stein, ed., 1977.

Works of Edwards not included in the present editions of Edwards' collected works are:

Images and Shadows of Divine Things. Perry Miller, ed., New Haven: Yale University Press, 1948.

Charity and Its Fruits. Tryon Edwards, ed., New London, Conn.: 1851. Reprinted by the Banner of Truth Trust, London: 1969.

The Philosophy of Jonathan Edwards: From his Private Notebooks. H. G. Townsend, ed., Eugene Ore: University of Oregon Press, 1955.

Treatise on Grace. Paul Helm, ed., Cambridge: James Clarke & Co. Ltd, 1971.

Introductions to the life and thought of Edwards:

Cherry, Conrad. The Theology of Jonathan Edwards: a Reappraisal. Garden City, N.Y.: Doubleday and Co., Anchor Books, 1966.

Delattre, Roland A. <u>Beauty and Sensibility in the Thought of</u>
<u>Jonathan Edwards</u>. New Haven: Yale University Press, 1968.

Elwood, Douglas J. <u>The Philosophical Theology of Jonathan</u>
<u>Edwards</u>. New York: Columbia University Press, 1960.

<u>Jonathan Edwards: Selections</u>. C. H. Faust & T. H. Johnson.
New York: Hill and Wang, 1962. This edition of selections
from Edwards is the best anthology of his works available,
contains excellent and thorough introductions, and has a
fine annotated bibliography which has entries from as
late as 1961.

Perry Miller. <u>Jonathan Edwards</u>. New York: Dell Publishing
Co., a Delta Book, 1949.

Winslow, Ola E. <u>Jonathan Edwards</u>. New York: Macmillian,
1941.

Index

About the Author

Patricia Wilson-Kastner is presently Associate Professor of Historical and Constructive Theology at United Theological Seminary of the Twin Cities. She was born in 1944 in New York City; her family moved to Texas shortly thereafter. She did undergraduate work in English at the University of Dallas, graduating with a B.A. in 1967, and receiving an M.A. in Theology from the same institution in 1969, having taken out a year to teach high school. In 1973 she was awarded the Ph.D. in Religion by the University of Iowa. During her time in Iowa City she served as pastor of the Welsh Congregational Church for 1972-73, and lecturer in religion at Cornell College in Mt. Vernon, Iowa in spring of 1973. She was a Visiting Assistant Professor at United Seminary from 1973-74, when she left to go to Iceland with her husband, G. Ronald Kastner, who went there on a Fulbright Fellowship to work on his dissertation in Comparative Literature. In 1975 she returned to United Theological Seminary as director of the Doctor of Ministry program (1975-76) and Assistant Professor. She and her husband are now in St. Paul, where they are working together on a source book on women writers of the early church, and she is laboring on a study of the Greek background of Augustine of Hippo's theology of grace.